Mein erstes Wörterbuch

ENGLISCH

Lernspiele für die Grundschule

Hi, I'm Bobby. I'm from London.

Hi!
My name is ______________________

I'm from ______________________.

Klebe hier ein Foto ein oder male dich selbst.

EDITION BÜCHERBÄR

Animals on the farm

cat

The cat is chasing
a mouse.

duck

Ducks live near the
water.

cow

The cow gives us milk.

fly

There are a lot of flies
on the cake.

dog

The dog is barking.

goose

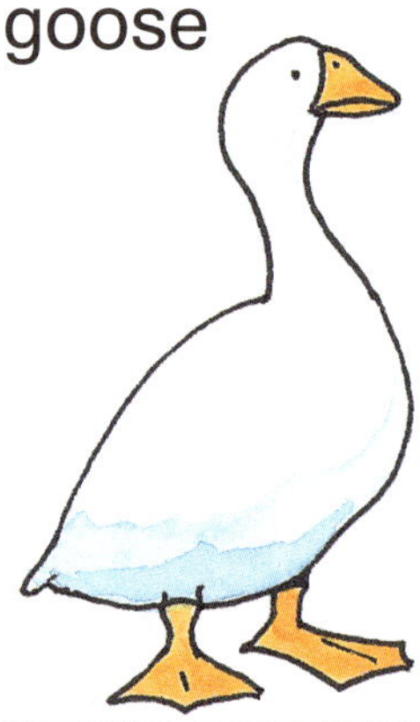

The goose is a kind of
bird.

Tiere auf dem Bauernhof

hen

The hen gives us eggs.

pig

Pigs have curly tails.

horse

Mary is sitting on a horse.

rabbit

The rabbit has long ears.

mouse

The mouse is afraid of the cat.

sheep

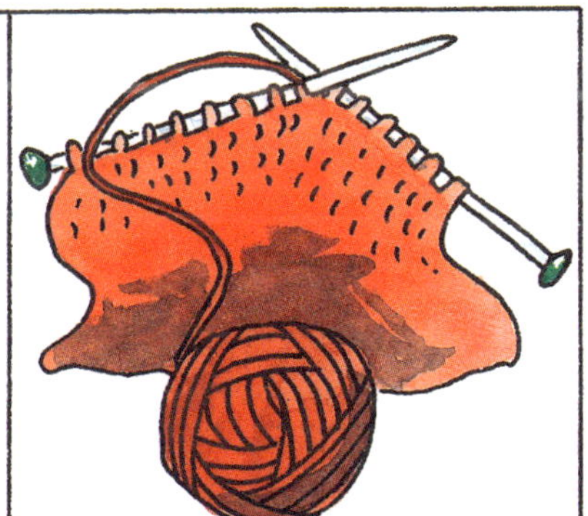

We get wool from sheep.

Animals on the farm

What goes with what?

Was gehört zusammen?

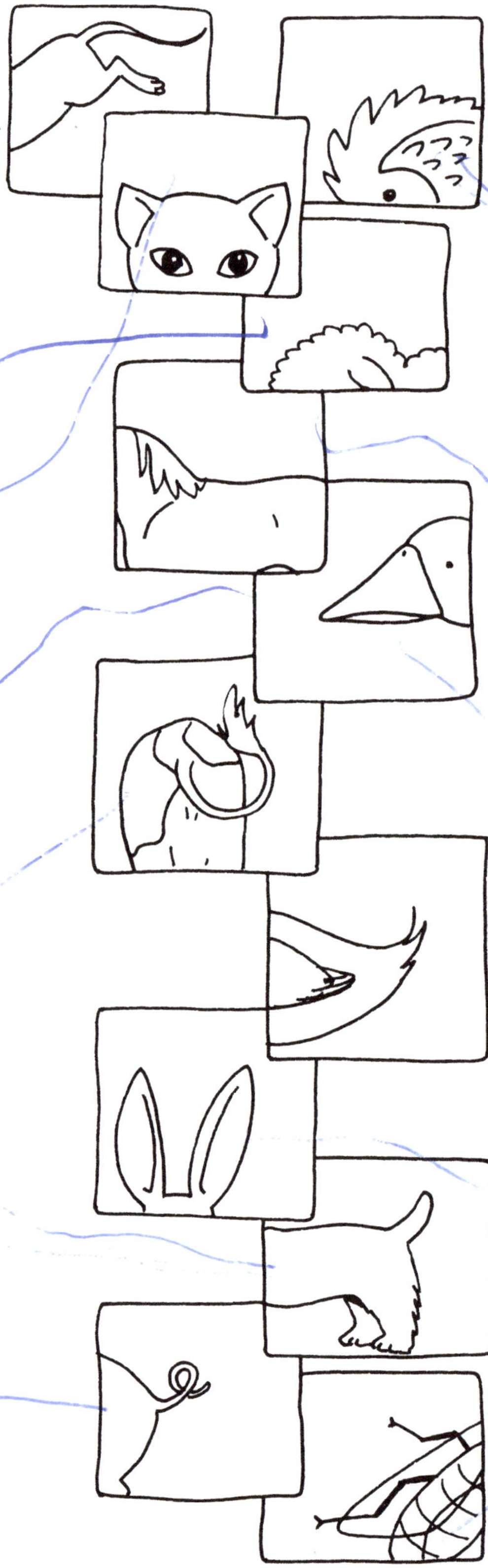

mouse

sheep

cat

goose

cow

dog

pig

hen

horse

rabbit

duck

fly

Tiere auf dem Bauernhof

What animals are hiding here? Put a cross in the correct box.

Welche fünf Tiere haben sich hier versteckt? Kreuze an!

cow	pig	cat	horse	rabbit	duck	hen

Who lives here? Put a cross in the correct box.

Wer wohnt hier? Kreuze an!

- [x] dog
- [ ] cow

- [ ] rabbit
- [x] mouse

- [ ] sheep
- [x] cat

- [x] hen
- [ ] fly

- [ ] pig
- [x] duck

- [x] horse
- [ ] goose

Animals in the zoo

bear

The bear is a wild animal.

giraffe

The giraffe has a long neck.

dolphin

The dolphin lives in the ocean.

lion

The lion is the king of the animals.

elephant

Elephants live in Africa.

monkey

Monkeys eat bananas.

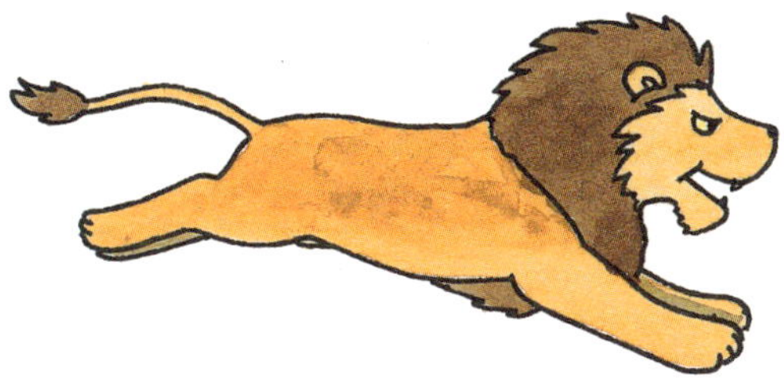

Tiere im Zoo

parrot

Parrots can talk.

snake

Snakes have no legs.

penguin

The penguin lives in the Antarctic.

tiger

A tiger is a big wild cat.

rhinoceros

This animal has one or two horns on its nose.

tortoise

Tortoises have shells.

Animals in the zoo

Do you recognize these animals?
Join up.

Erkennst du die Tiere?
Verbinde!

What do you know?

Was kennst du?

Musical instruments — Musikinstrumente

drum

Charly can play the drum.

piano

Nancy can play the piano.

guitar

Sally can play the guitar.

recorder

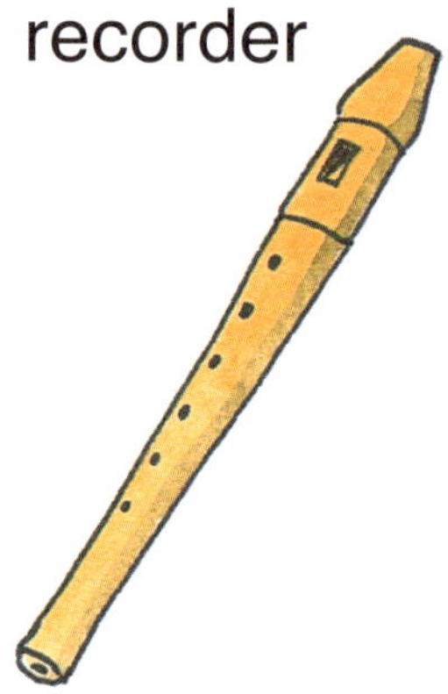

Lucy can play the recorder.

keyboard

John can play the keyboard.

trumpet

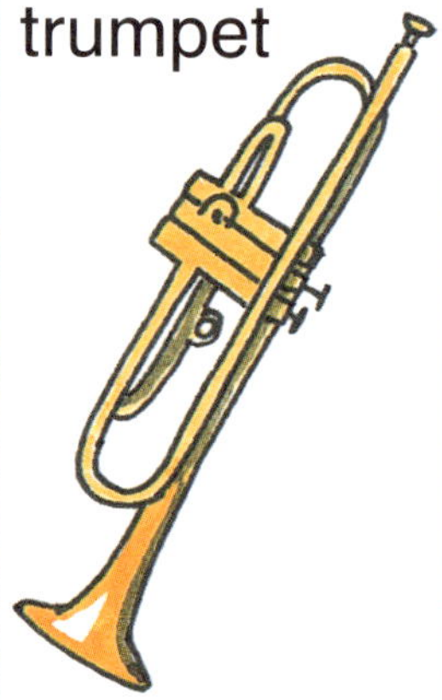

Alan can play the trumpet.

11 Toys — Spielzeuge

doll

Mary loves her doll.

skipping rope

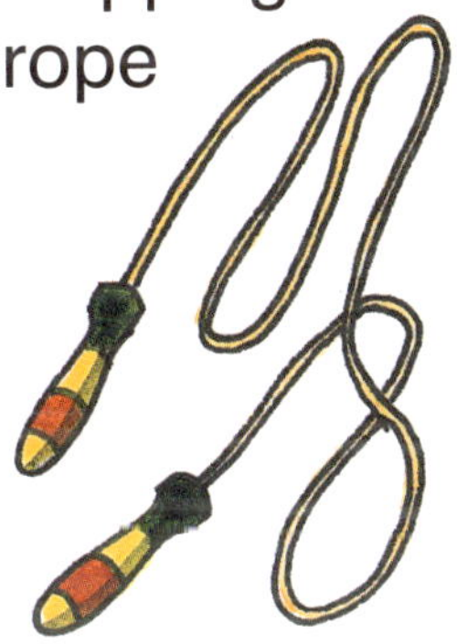

Helen and her skipping rope

jigsaw

Mabel and her jigsaw

teddy bear

Brian loves his teddy bear.

kite

Patrick and his kite

train set

Freddy plays with his train set.

Musical instruments

Musikinstrumente

Who can play what?

Wer spielt auf welchem Instrument?

piano

guitar

drum

keyboard

recorder

trumpet

What instrument can you play?

Welches Instrument kannst du spielen? Kreuze an.

13 Toys — Spielzeug

Who gets what?

Wer bekommt was?

The first letter of each child´s name will help you find his/her toy. Who gets nothing?

Die Anfangsbuchstaben der Kinder und der Spielsachen helfen dir weiter. Wer bekommt nichts?

What do you like playing with? Draw it.

Womit spielst du gerne? Male es.

one

There is only one earth.

two

I have two eyes.

three

Good luck!

four

Two and two are four.

five

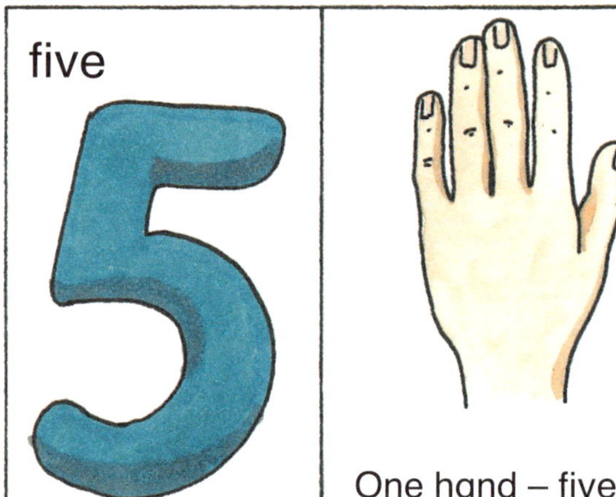

One hand – five fingers

six

Three and three are six.

seven

Snow White and the seven dwarfs

ten

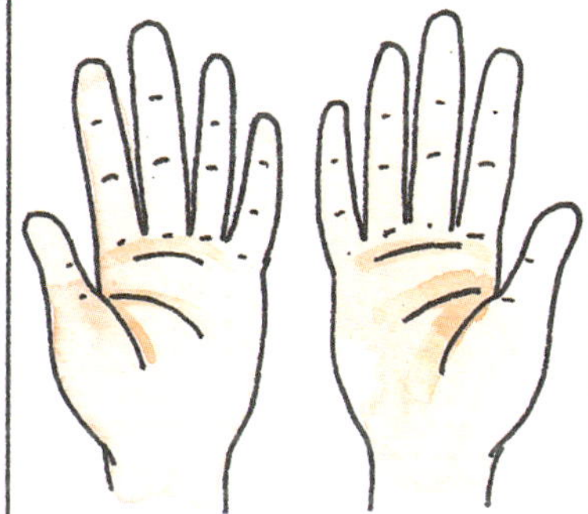

Two hands – ten fingers

eight

Four and four are eight.

zero

Zero! And the rocket takes off!

nine

This is a game of nine pins.

hundred

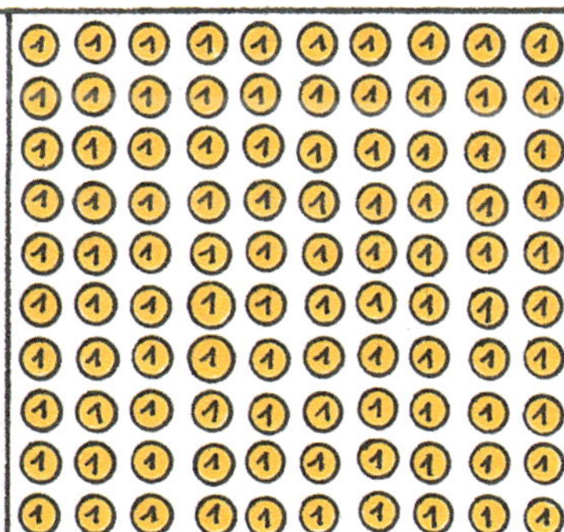

One Euro is the same as hundred cents.

Numbers

Count the animals. Zähle die Tiere!

Rearrange the letters. Ordne die Buchstaben!

0 1 2 3 4 5 6 7 8 9 10

orez	zero
evif	
neves	
eerht	
xis	
enin	

ten	nte
	owt
	ruof
	thgie
	eno

Join the numbers in the correct order. Verbinde die Zahlen der Reihe nach!

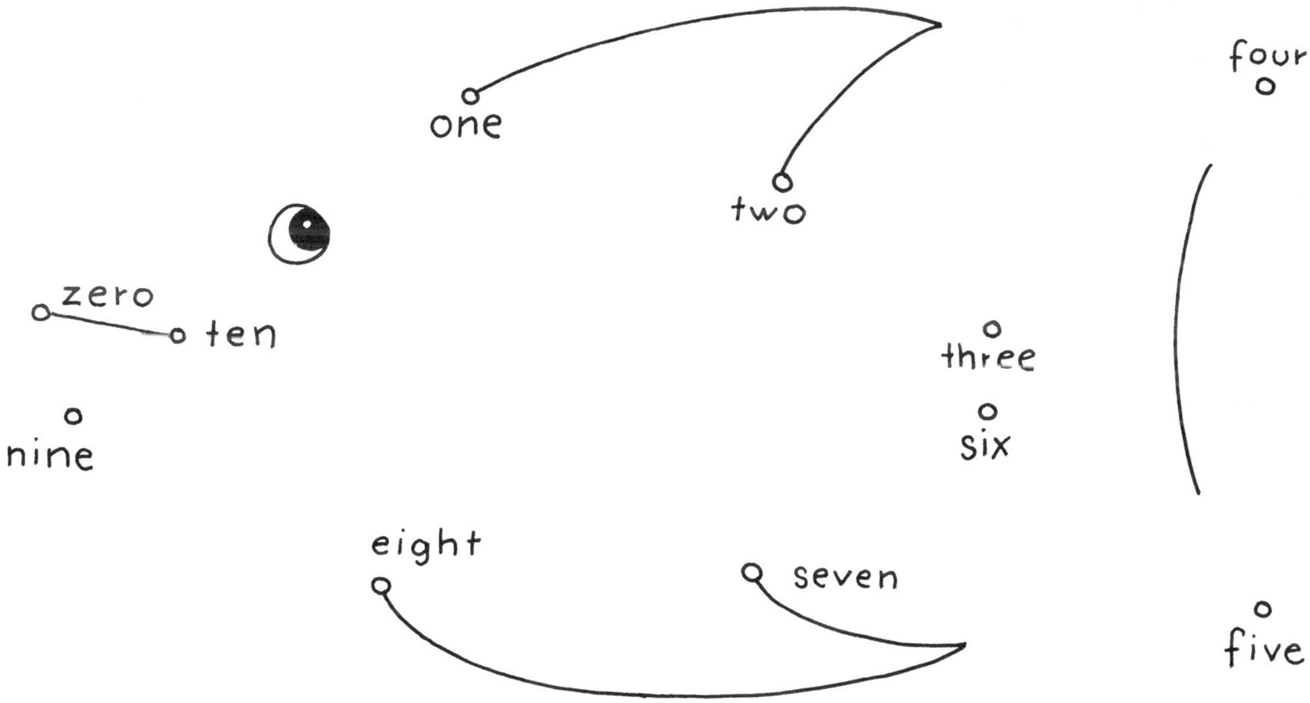

Complete the words. Ergänze die Zahlwörter!

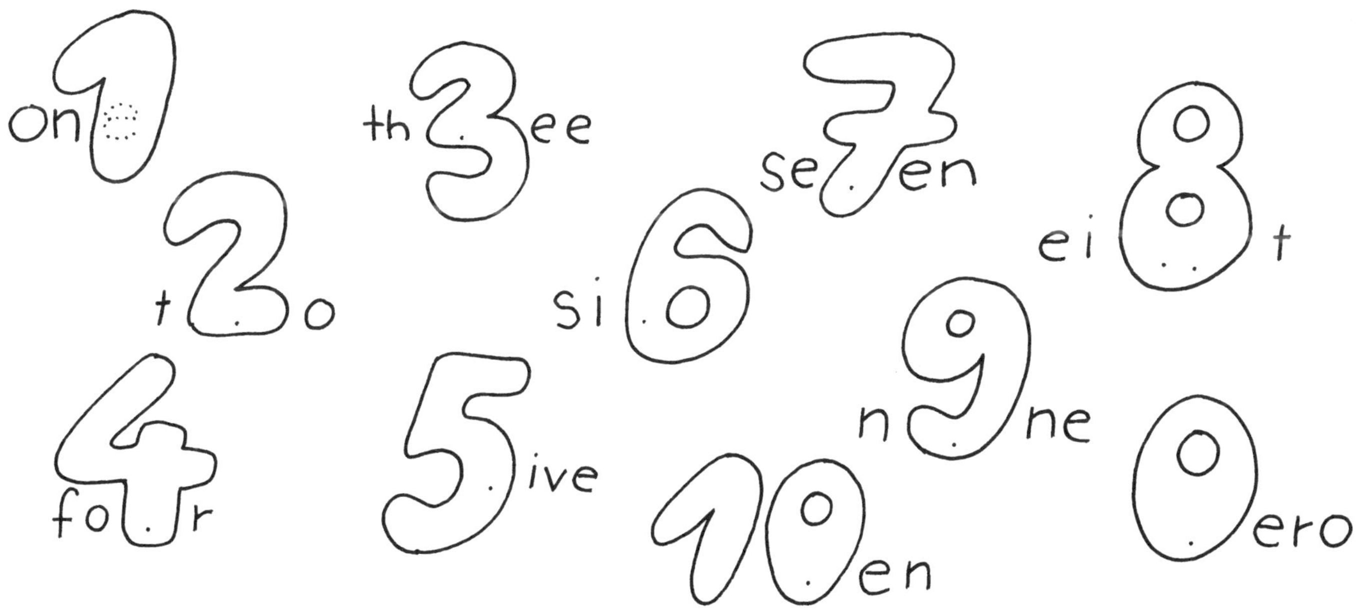

Colours

black

This bird is black.

green

The tree is green.

blue

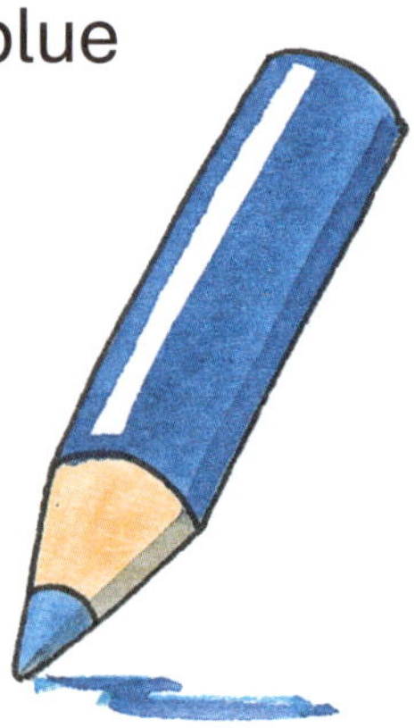

Water is blue.

grey

Clouds are grey.

brown

Most bears are brown.

orange

A carrot is orange.

Farben

pink

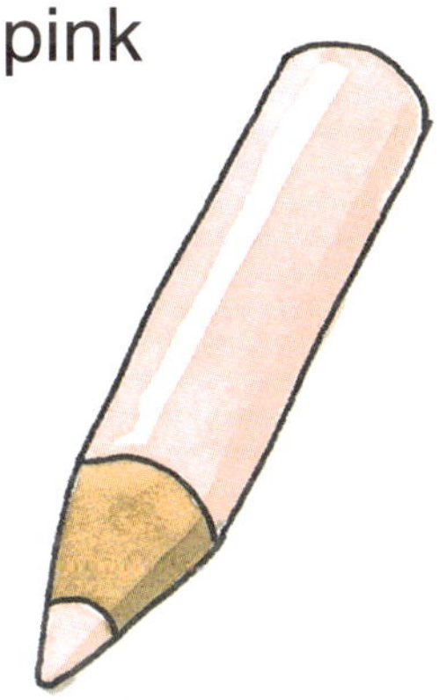

Pigs are usually pink.

white

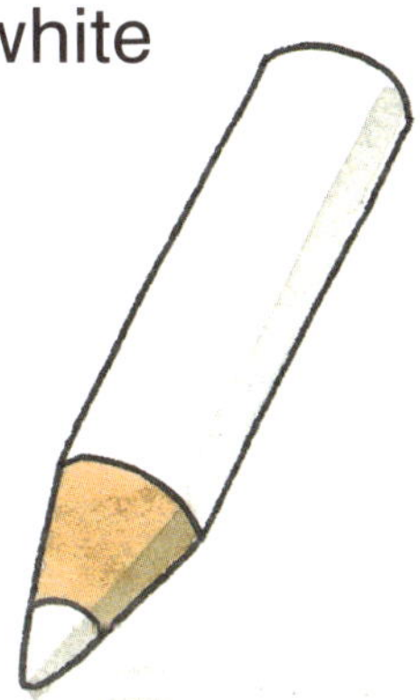

Snow is white.

purple

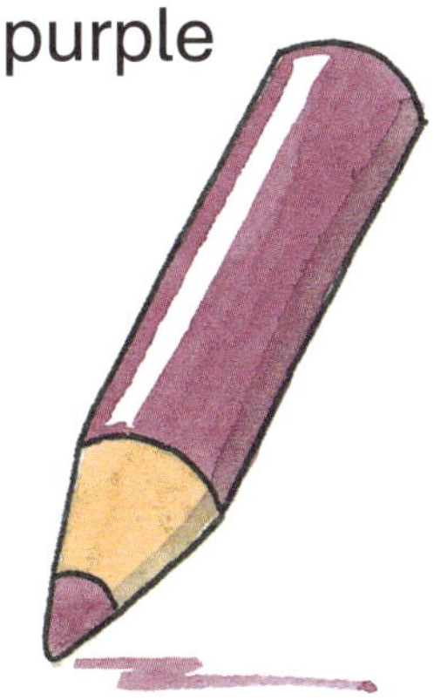

This flower is purple.

yellow

This fruit is yellow.

red

The tomato is red.

all together

Colours

Find the right colour.
Put a cross in the correct box.

Suche die richtige Farbe!
Kreuze an!

white
grey

yellow
red

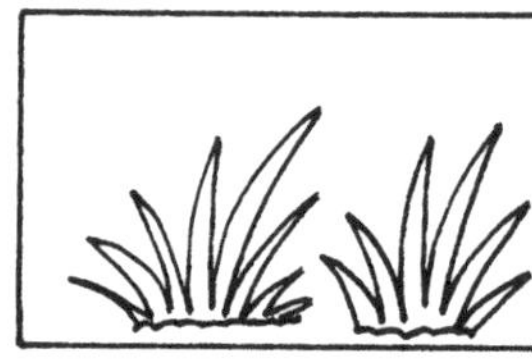
green
black

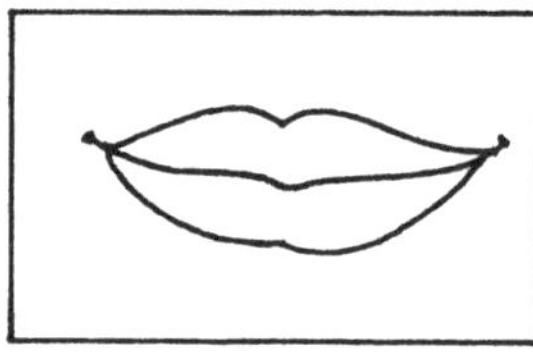
blue
red

white
pink

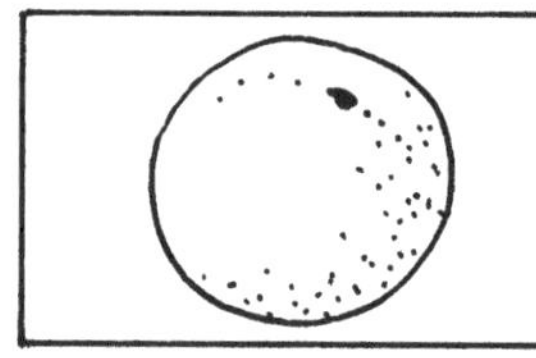
green
orange

black
purple

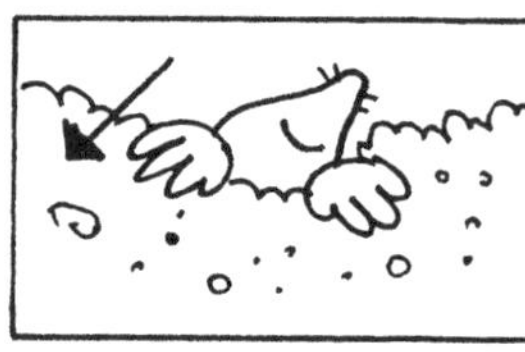
brown
red

grey
blue

Right or wrong?

Richtig oder falsch?

Put a cross on the correct face!

Kreuze an!

It is white.

It is green.

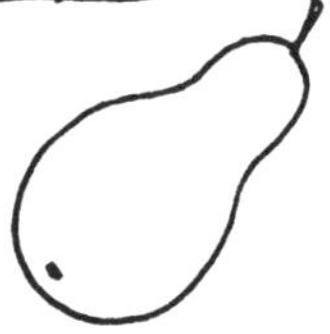
It is purple.

It is grey.

It is blue.

It is red.

Colour this picture correctly.

Male richtig an!

1 pink	4 yellow	7 purple
2 red	5 green	8 grey
3 blue	6 brown	9 orange

School things

board

I can write on the board.

exercise book

I can write in my exercise book.

book

There are a lot of books in my school bag.

glue

I can stick bits of paper together with glue.

crayon

I can colour a picture with crayons.

notebook

I can write in my notebook.

Schulsachen

pen

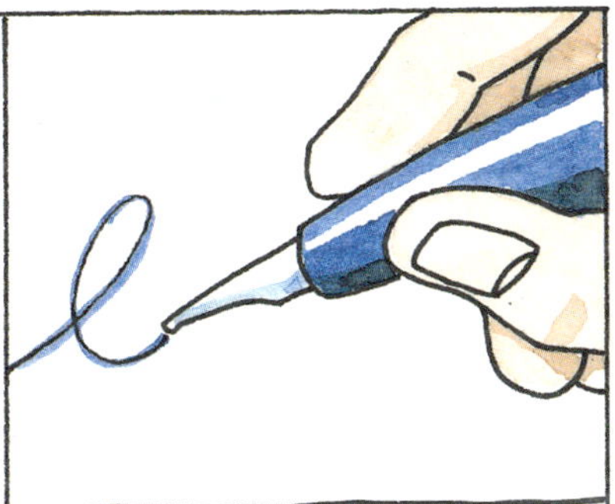

I can write with my pen.

ruler

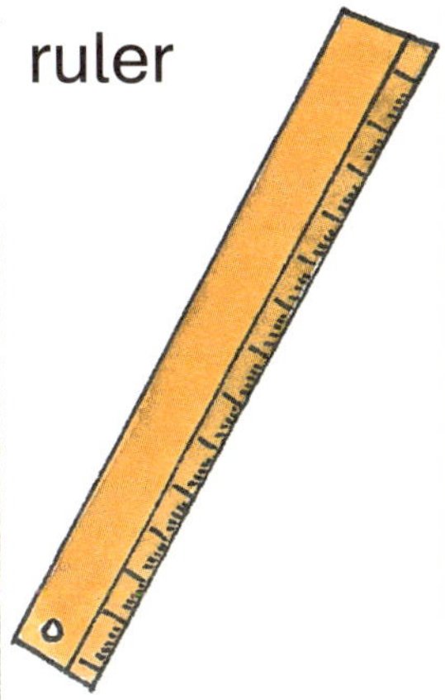

I can draw lines with my ruler.

pencil

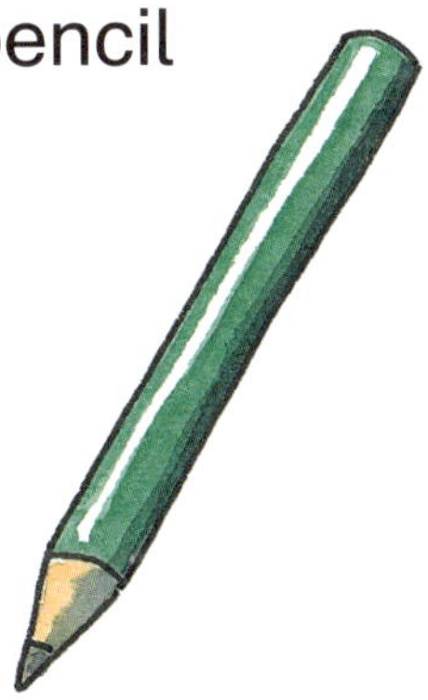

I can write with my pencil.

school bag

I must carry my school bag.

rubber

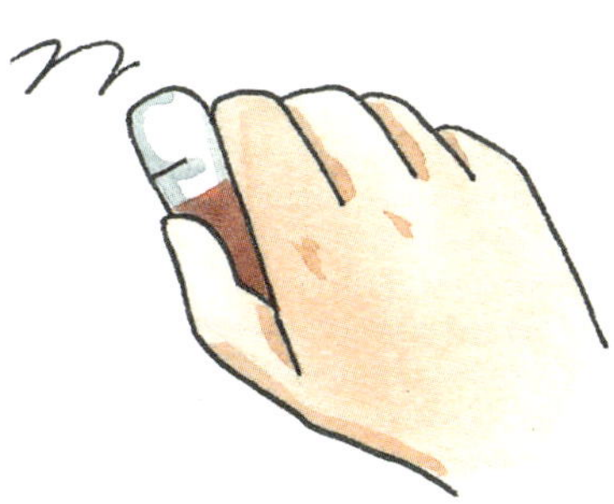

When I make a mistake I use my rubber.

scissors

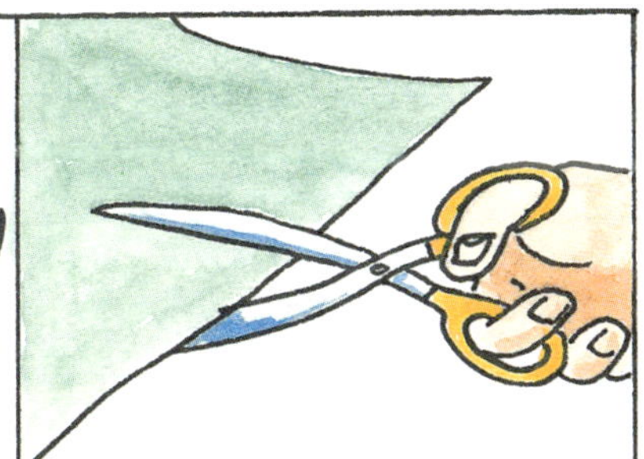

I can cut with my scissors.

School things

What words are written on the crayons? Wie heißen die Wörter auf den Stiften?

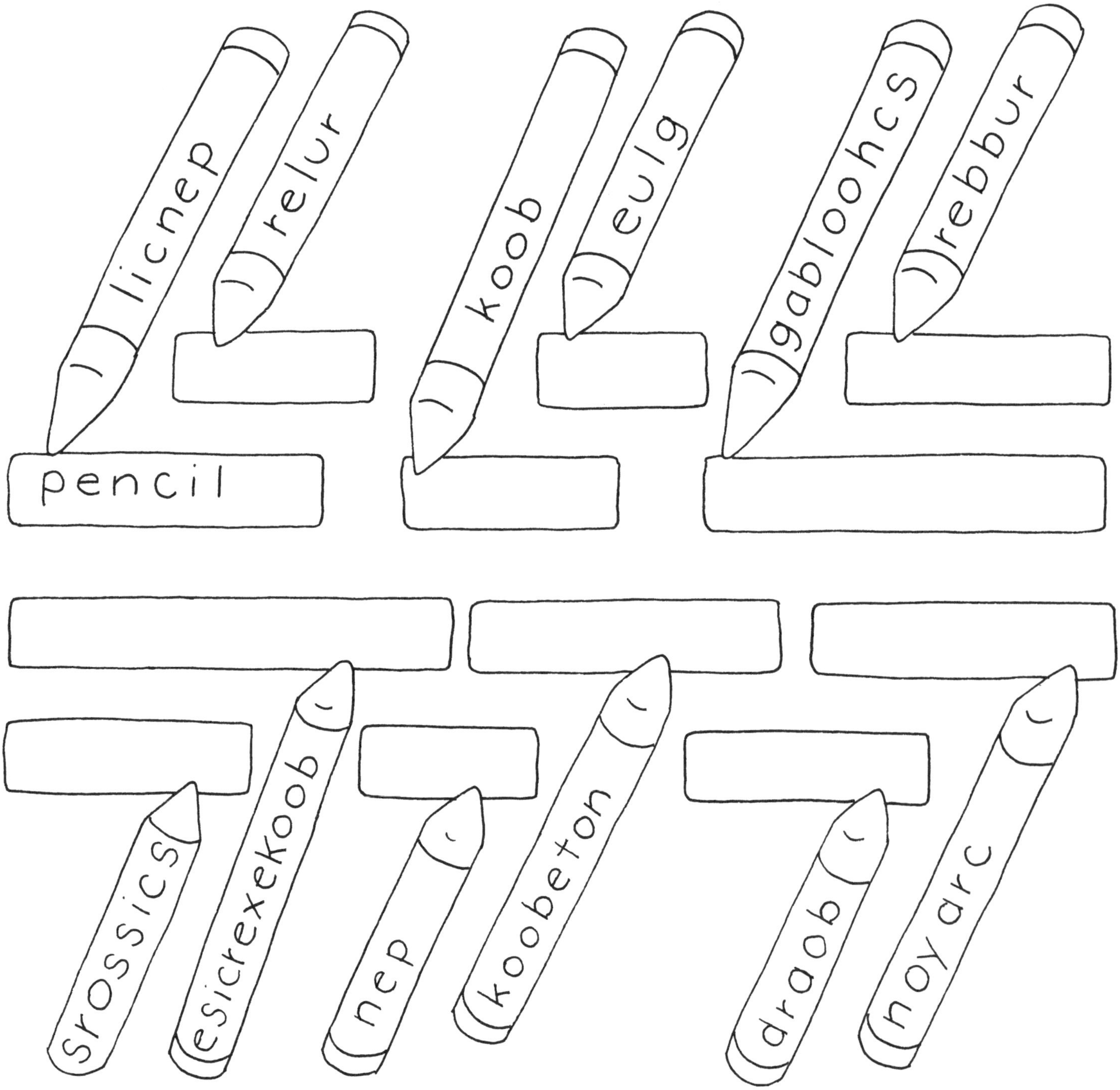

What a mess!

Welches Durcheinander!

John is trying to find his school things in his room.

John sucht seine Schulsachen in seinem Zimmer.

Fill in the correct number.

Trage die richtige Zahl ein!

○ pencil ○ book ○ pen ○ notebook ○ school bag

○ scissors ○ ruler ○ glue ○ crayon ○ rubber

apple

An apple is yellow, red or green.

grapes

Wine is made from grapes.

banana

Monkeys like bananas.

kiwi fruit

A kiwi fruit has a lot of vitamins.

cherry

Cherries are red.

lemon

Lemons are sour.

orange

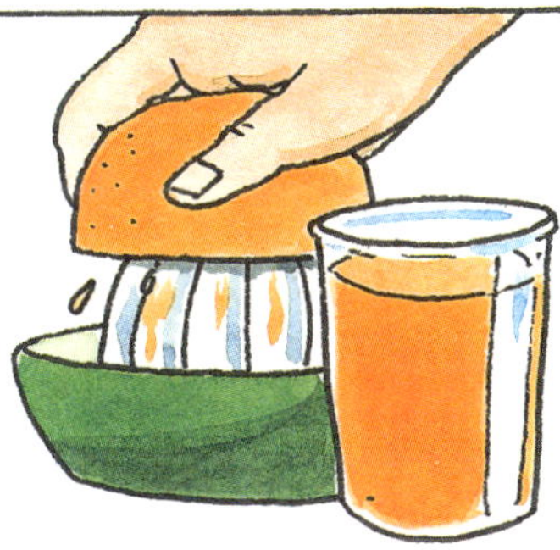

An orange is a juicy fruit.

pineapple

A pineapple is sweet.

peach

A peach is very juicy.

strawberry

I like strawberry ice cream.

pear

A pear is yellow or green.

water melon

A water melon is a big fruit.

Bobby likes to eat ... Bobby isst gerne . . .

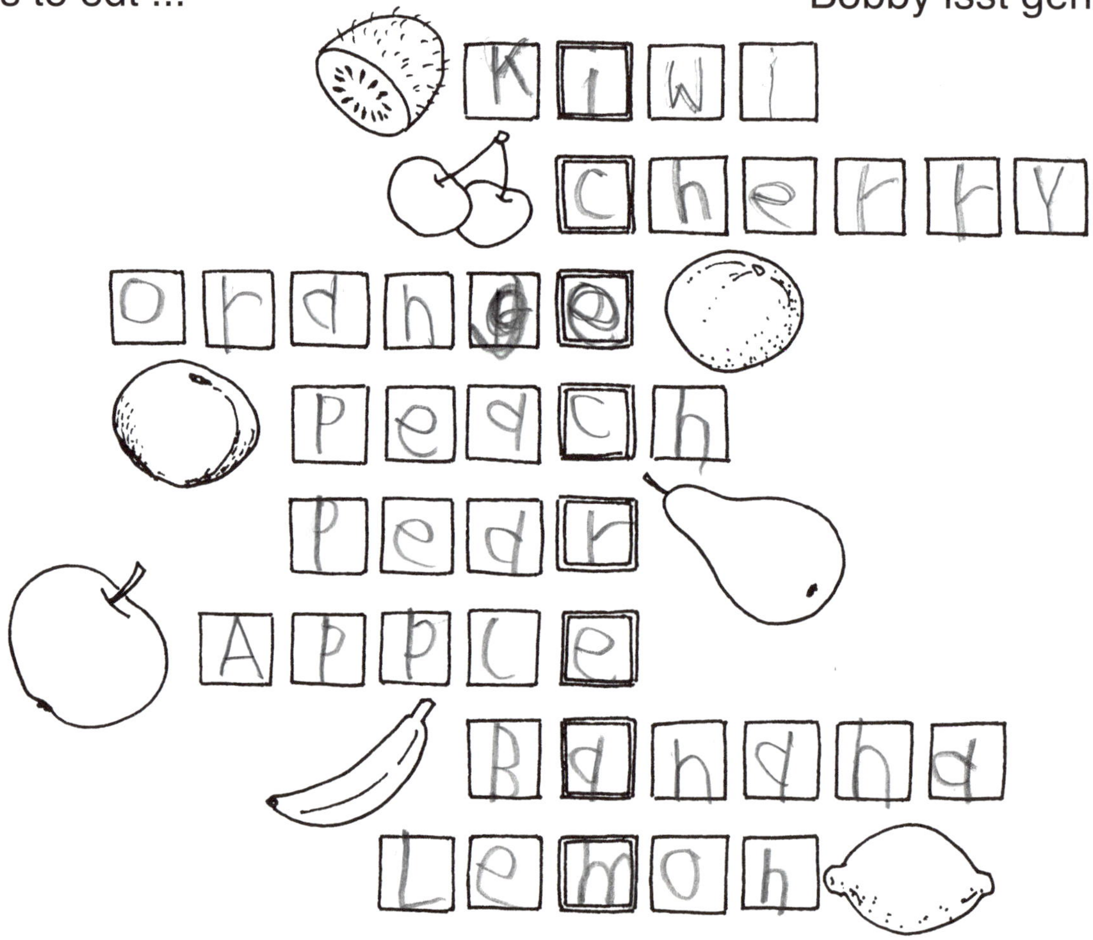

Draw it here. Male!

A magic tree –
do you know all the fruits?

Ein Wunderbaum –
Kennst du alle Früchte?

Join up.

Ziehe Linien!

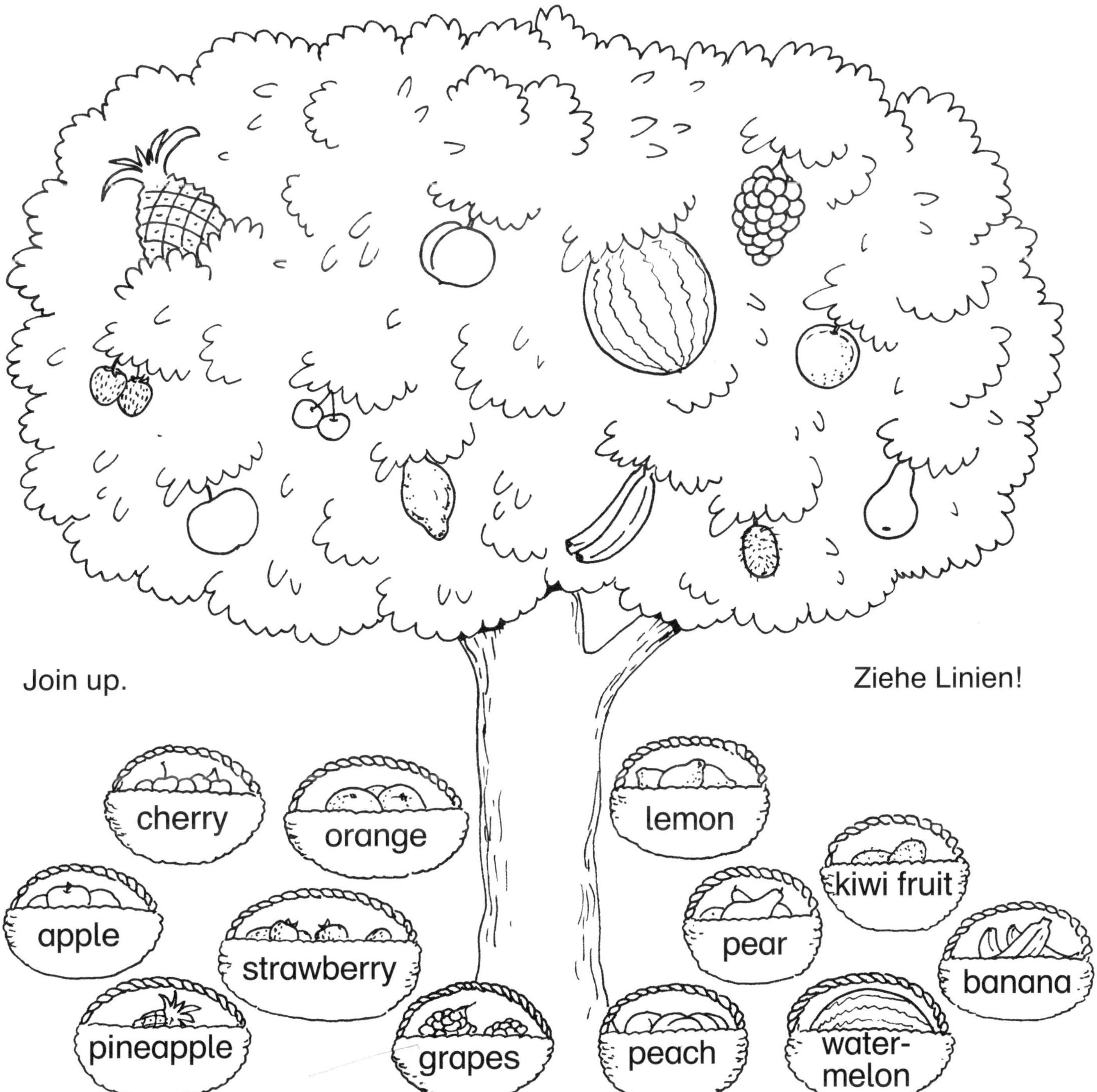

Vehicles

bike

I can ride a bike.

car

I´m going by car.

boat

This is a little boat.

helicopter

The helicopter is landing on the ground.

bus

I´m going by bus.

motorbike

I can´t ride a motorbike.

plane

The plane is flying through the sky.

taxi

This taxi is going slowly.

scooter

Tommy likes going on his scooter.

train

This train is going fast.

ship

This is a big ship.

tram

You go round the town by tram.

Vehicles

Put the words into the correct groups. Ordne richtig zu!

taxi

car

bus

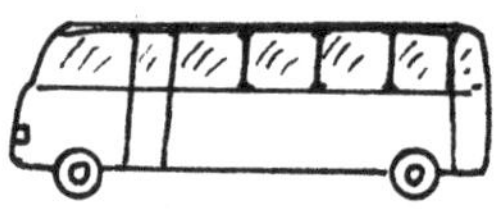

scooter

bike

motorbike

plane

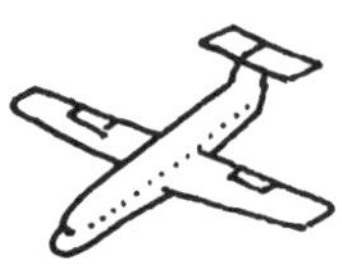

boat

ship

helicopter

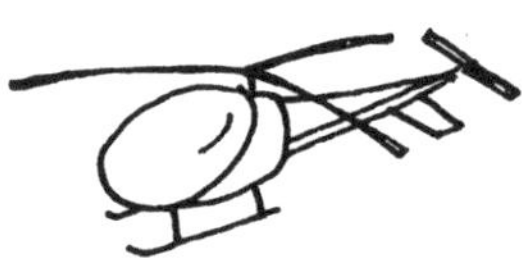

tram

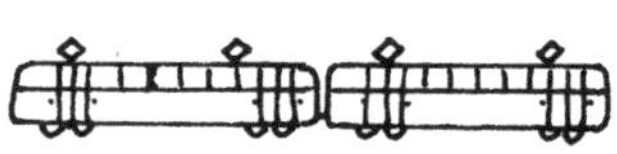

two wheels

four wheels

in the air

on the water

What is left? Draw it.
Was bleibt übrig? Male!

What is hidden in this picture?

Was hat sich hier versteckt?

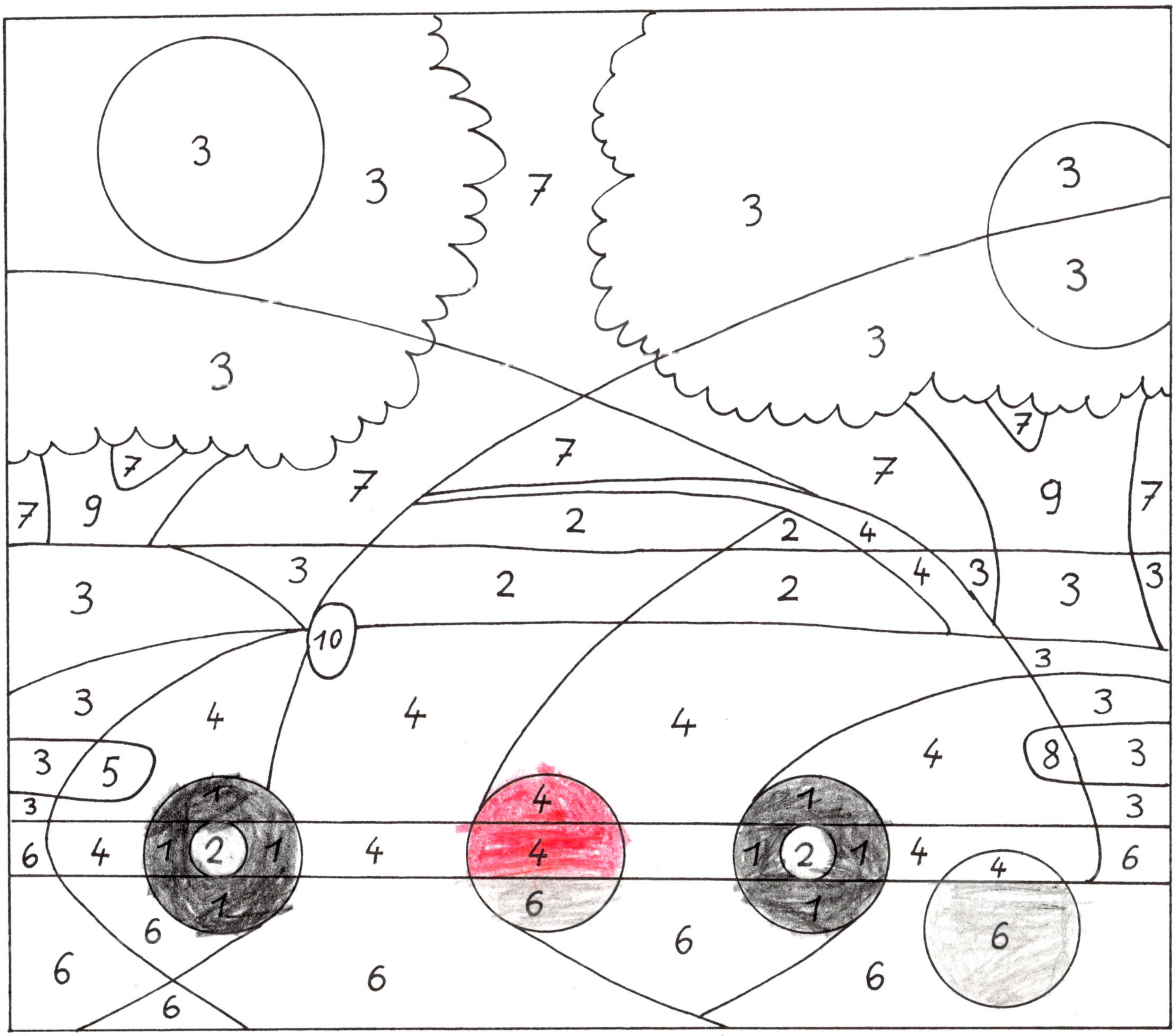

1 black, 2 white, 3 green, 4 red, 5 yellow, 6 grey, 7 blue, 8 orange, 9 brown, 10 pink

Food

bread and butter

John is eating bread and butter.

fish and chips

Fish and chips is a typical British meal.

cake

This is my birthday cake.

ham and cheese

Kevin loves ham and cheese sandwiches.

egg

The hen lays an egg every day.

jam and honey

I like bread and jam and bread and honey.

sausages

The butcher sells sausages.

breakfast

It´s breakfast time.

spaghetti and pizza

The children are eating spaghetti and pizza.

lunch

It´s lunch time.

soup

Freddy doesn´t like soup.

dinner

It´s dinner time.

At a restaurant

What's on the menu?

Start with ◯.

Im Restaurant

Wie heißen die Gerichte auf der Speisekarte?
Beginne mit ◯!

Menu

b r d e a		g e g	
p a i zz		ch s ee e	
j m a		h n o e y	
sp e gh a tti		s p ou	
s s a e au g		c k a e	
f i s h		ch s i p	

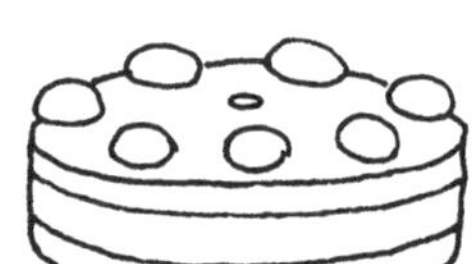

Who is eating what?
Look at the first letter of the names.
Draw the food on the plate.

Wer isst was? Schau auf den gemeinsamen Anfangsbuchstaben. Male das Essen auf den Teller!

Things to drink

beer

Father likes to drink beer.

coke

Many people like to drink coke.

champagne

Some people like to drink champagne.

fizzy water

Sally is drinking fizzy water.

coffee

Mother likes to drink coffee.

hot chocolate

Sandy likes to drink hot chocolate.

Getränke

juice

Tom likes to drink juice.

tea

Grandma likes to drink tea.

lemonade

Henry likes to drink lemonade.

whisky

Mr. Thompson likes to drink whisky.

milk

I like to drink milk.

wine

Grandfather likes to drink wine.

Things to drink

Put in the right column. Ordne richtig!

☺ good for children ☹ bad for children

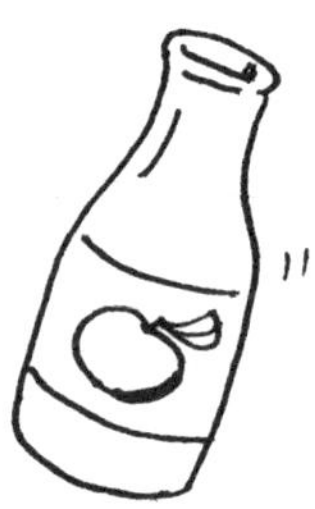

☹	coffee	4
	coke	2
	fizzy water	1
	wine	
	champagne	8
	juice	3
	lemonade	6
	milk	9
	whisky	5
	beer	10
	hot chocolate	
	tea	7

Bobby likes to drink ...

Check the numbers and write the names of the drinks in the correct place.

Was Bobby gerne trinkt ....

Vergleiche die Nummern der Getränke von der vorigen Seite und schreibe die Namen an die richtige Stelle.

father

This is Mr. Brown.
He is the father.

mother

This is Mrs. Brown.
She is the mother.

son

This is Bobby Brown.
He is the son.

daughter

This is Susan Brown.
She is the daughter.

brother

Bobby is Susan´s brother.

sister

Susan is Bobby´s sister.

Bobbys Familie

grandfather

This is Bobby´s and Susan´s grandfather. He is Mr. Brown´s father.

grandmother

This is Bobby´s and Susan´s grandmother. She is Mr. Brown´s mother.

uncle

This is Uncle John, Mr. Brown´s brother.

aunt

This is Aunt Lucy, Mr. Brown´s sister.

baby

This is the youngest child, Mary. She´s a baby.

children

Bobby, Susan and Mary are the Brown children.

Put into pairs.

Wer gehört zusammen? Immer ein Paar!

aunt

mother

grandfather

sister

grandmother

brother

uncle

father

Who is hiding behind the door?

Wer hat sich hinter der Tür versteckt? Schreibe auf!

Bobbys Familie

Who is who?

Familienfoto! Wer ist es?

- ◯ Susan
- ◯ Mother Brown
- ◯ Uncle John
- ◯ Aunt Lucy
- ◯ Father Brown
- ◯ Grand-father
- ◯ Grand-mother
- ◯ Bobby

asparagus

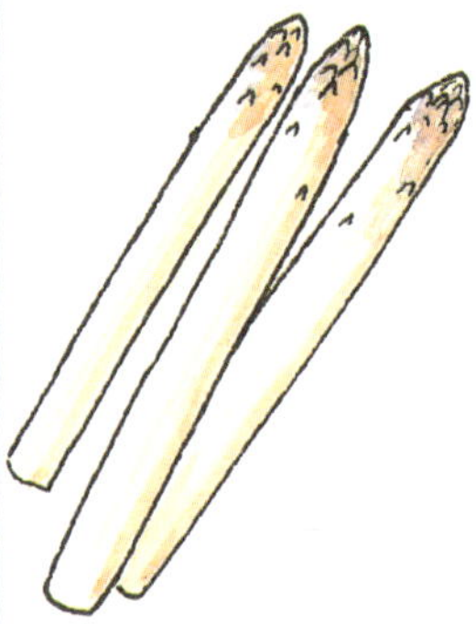

I like to eat asparagus with butter.

cauliflower

I don´t like to eat cauliflower.

broccoli

I like to eat broccoli soup.

courgettes

I like to eat courgette pie.

carrot

I like to eat grated carrots.

cucumber

I like to eat cucumber salad.

Gemüse

lettuce

My rabbit likes to eat lettuce.

potato

I like to eat potatoes.

mushroom

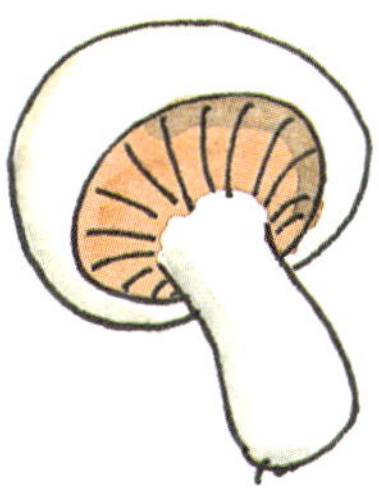

I like to eat mushrooms.

radishes

I don´t like radishes.

onion

I don´t like onions.

tomato

I can cook tomato soup.

Vegetables

What would you like to eat?

Was möchtest du essen?

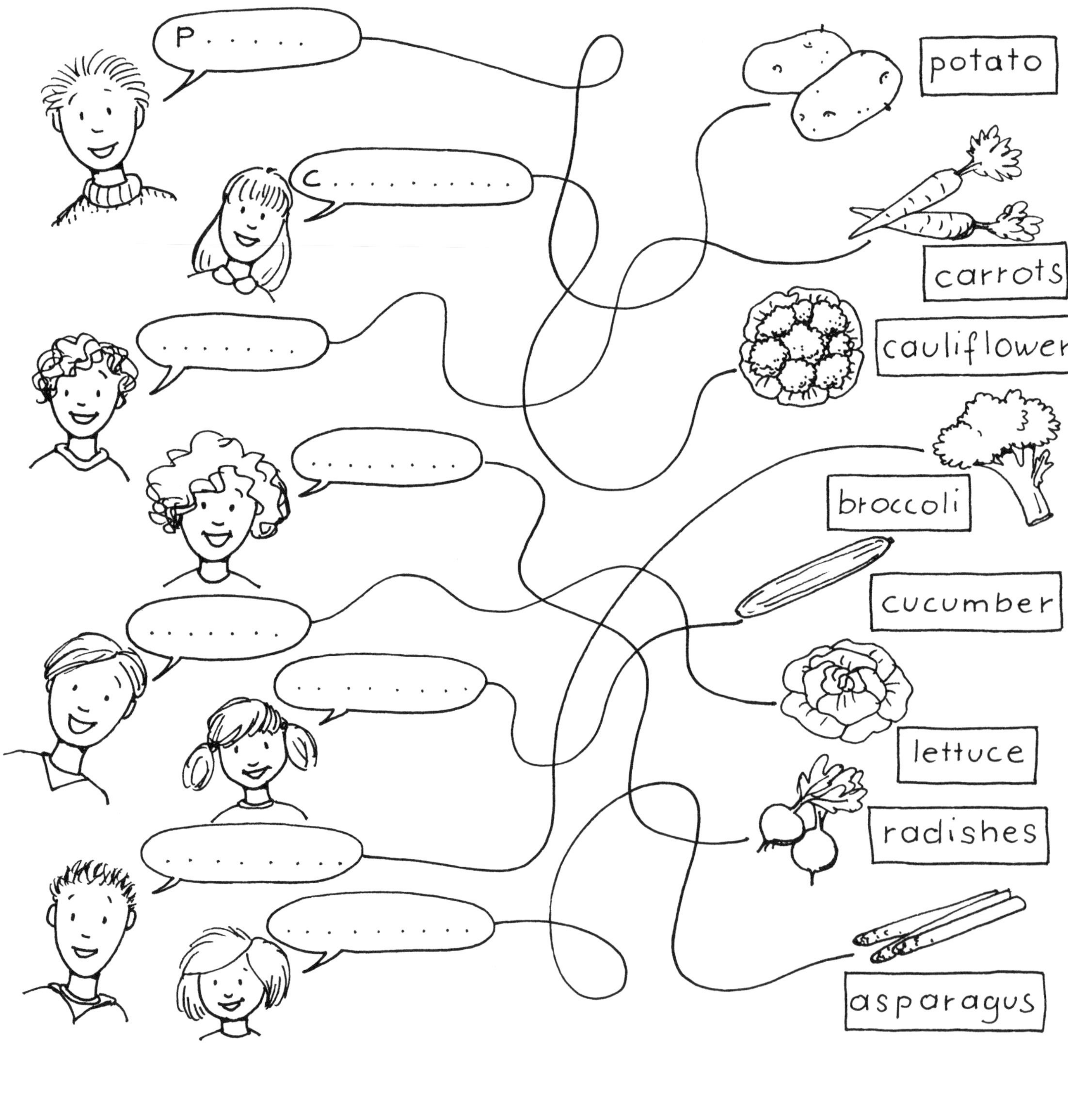

Gemüse

Letter salad
Join up.

Buchstabensalat
Verbinde!

bottle

The wine is in the bottle.

dishwasher

The dishwasher is full.

cooker

The saucepan is on the cooker.

fork

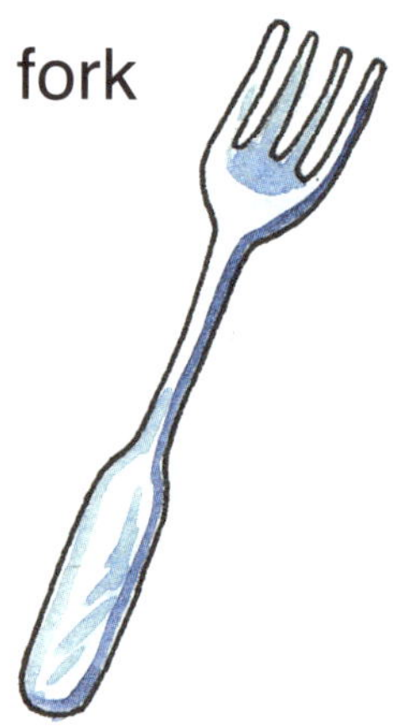

I eat spaghetti with a fork.

cup

Grandma is drinking a cup of tea.

fridge

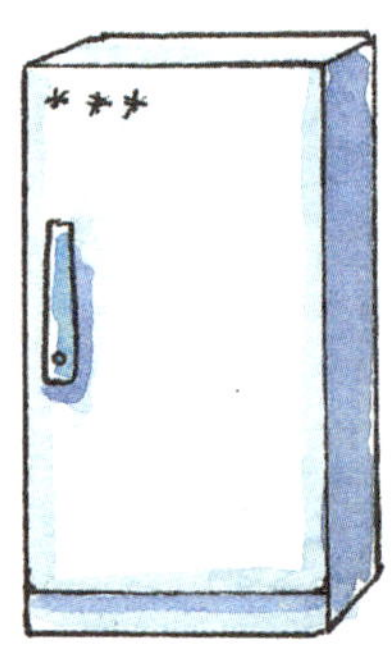

It is cold in the fridge.

In der Küche

glass

Dad is drinking a glass of wine.

spoon

I eat soup with a spoon.

knife

I cut bread with a knife.

teapot

The teapot is on the table.

plate

The food is on the plate.

toaster

You can toast bread in the toaster.

In the kitchen

Fill in the missing letters.
Now you know what Bobby likes to eat.

Welcher Buchstabe fehlt? Ergänze.
Nun weißt du, was Bobby mag.
Kreuze das passende Bild an!

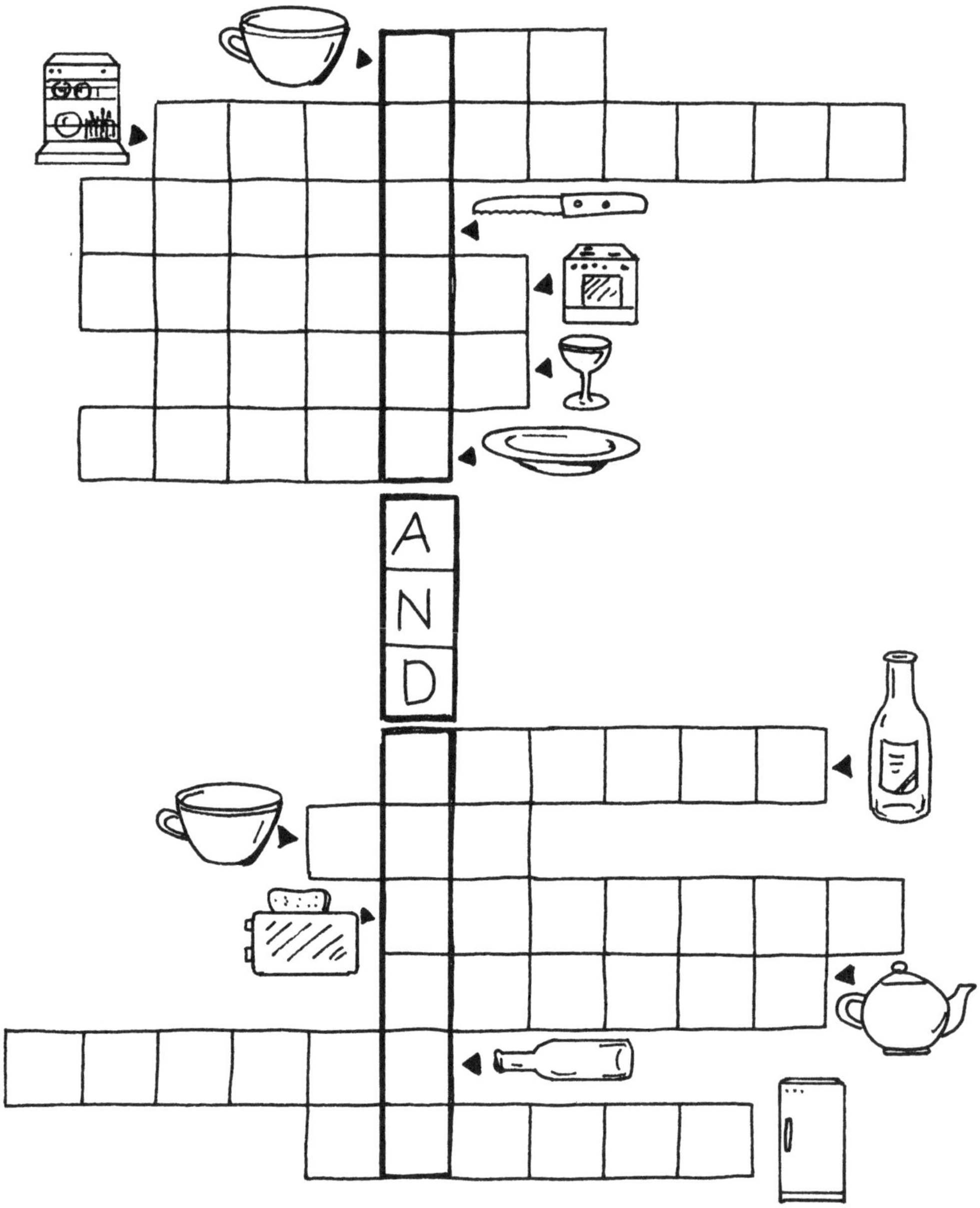

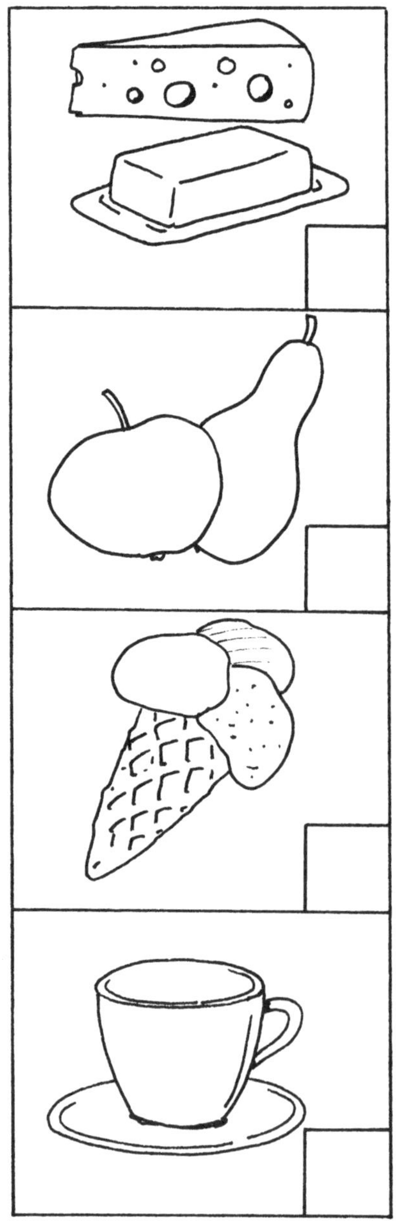

Letter salad
What belongs together?

Buchstabensalat
Was gehört zusammen?

Clothes

cardigan

My cardigan is blue.

jacket

Father has a green jacket.

coat

Grandma´s coat is warm.

shirt

This shirt is new.

dress

This is a nice dress.

shorts

John wears shorts in summer.

skirt

This is a white skirt.

trousers

Father has blue trousers.

socks

The socks are green.

umbrella

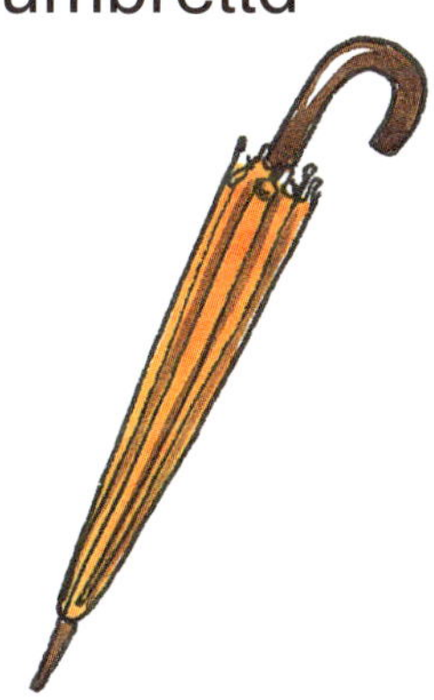

An umbrella keeps you dry when it rains.

sweater

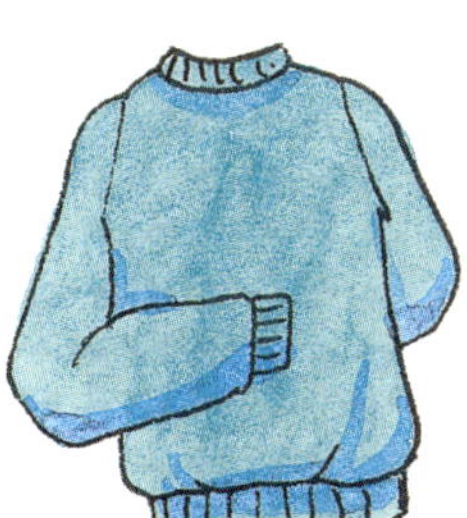

Monica has a new sweater.

underwear

This is Kevin´s underwear.

Clothes

Colour the clothes correctly.

Male richtig aus!

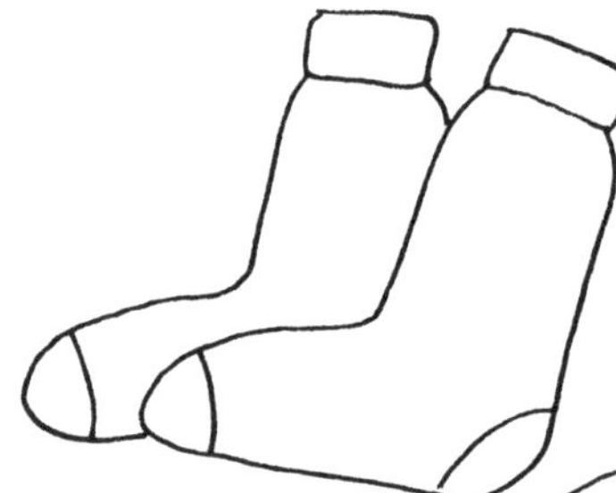

The coat is green.

The socks are red.

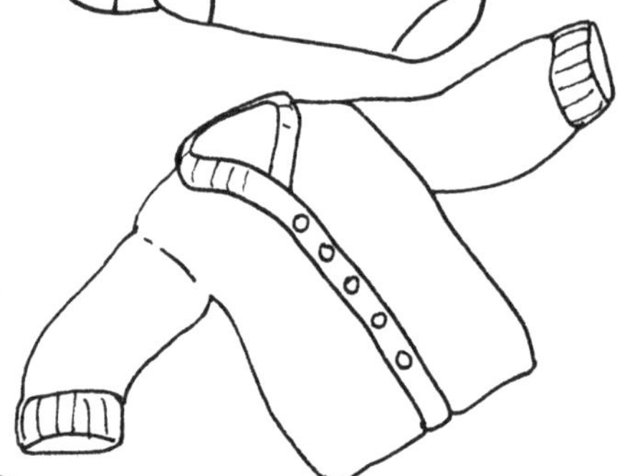

The trousers are blue.

The cardigan is brown.

The dress is pink.

The jacket is black.

The underwear is white.

The shirt is orange.

The sweater is yellow.

The shorts are white.

The skirt is purple.

The umbrella is multi-coloured.

Cross out the mistakes.

Etwas ist falsch. Streiche es weg!

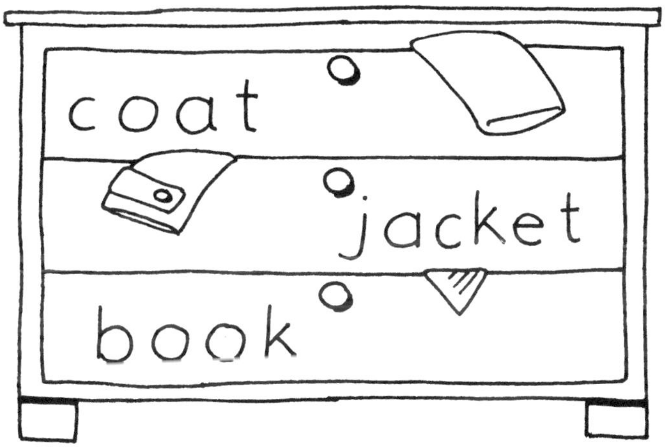

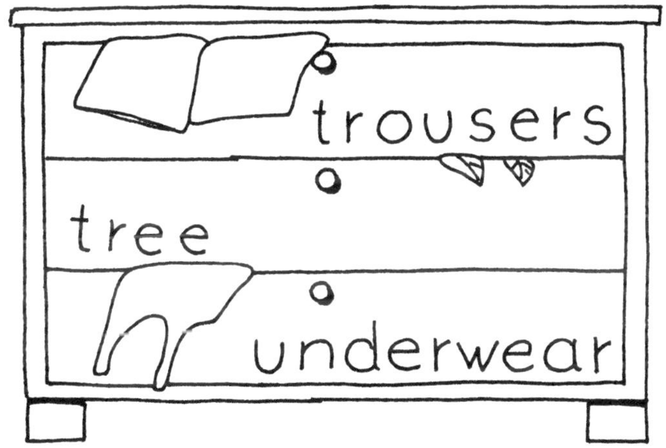

What do you like wearing best of all?
Draw it here.

Was trägst du am liebsten?
Male!

Clothes II

boots

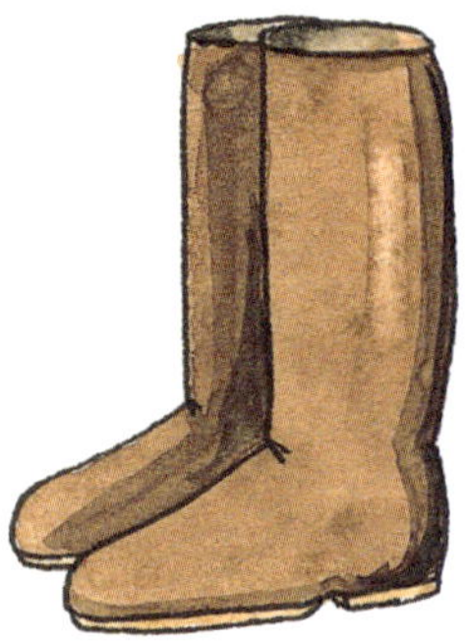

Susan has brown boots.

handbag

Mary´s handbag is big.

cap

Kevin has a blue cap.

hat

Tom´s hat is green.

glove

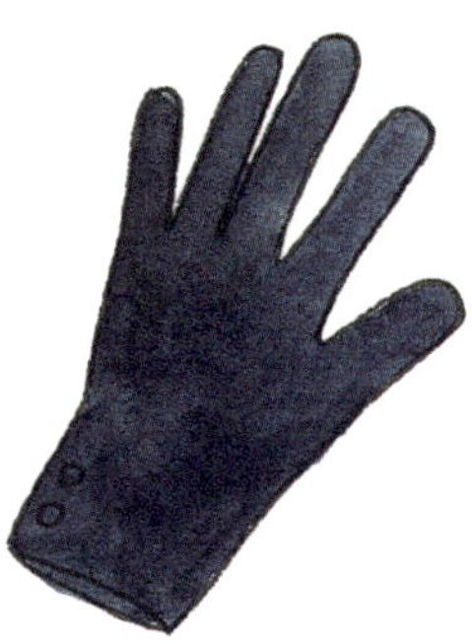

Grandmother has black gloves.

ring

Susan has a gold ring.

scarf

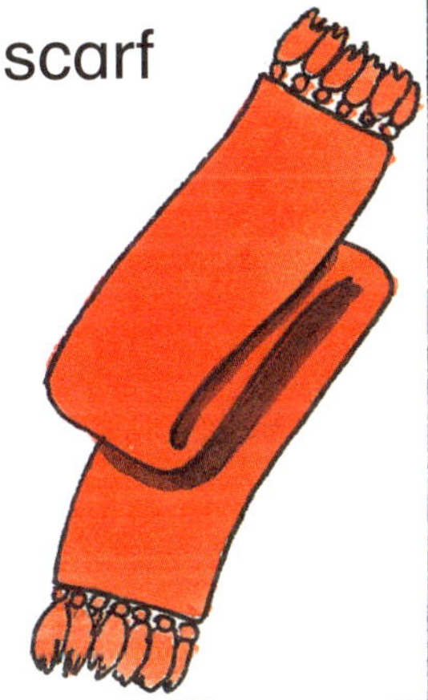

Mother has a red scarf.

sunglasses

Grandfather´s sunglasses are broken.

shoes

Tina has nice shoes.

tie

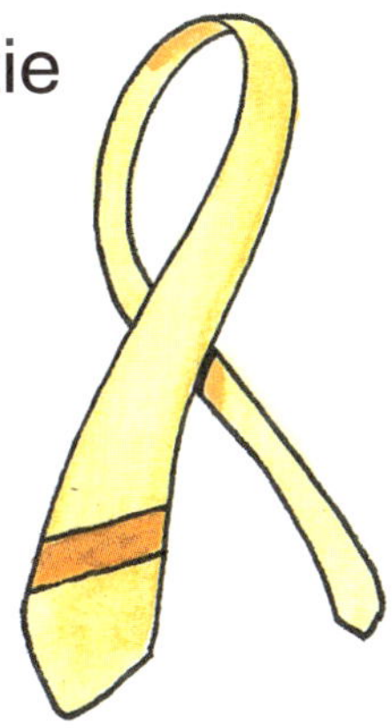

Father´s tie is new.

suitcase

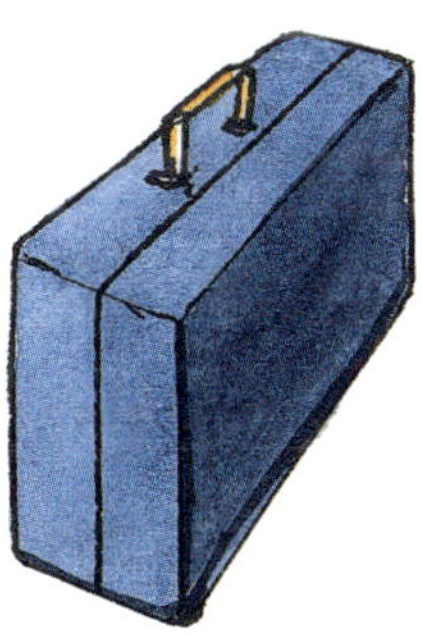

Fred´s suitcase has wheels.

watch

John has a silver watch.

What has Bobby put in his suitcase? Was hat Bobby in den Koffer gelegt?

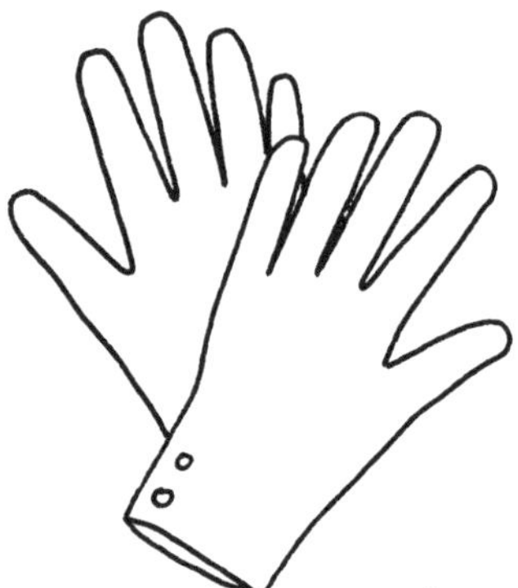

- gloves ○
- cap ○
- boots ○
- scarf ○
- tie ○
- watch ○
- ring ○
- shoes ○

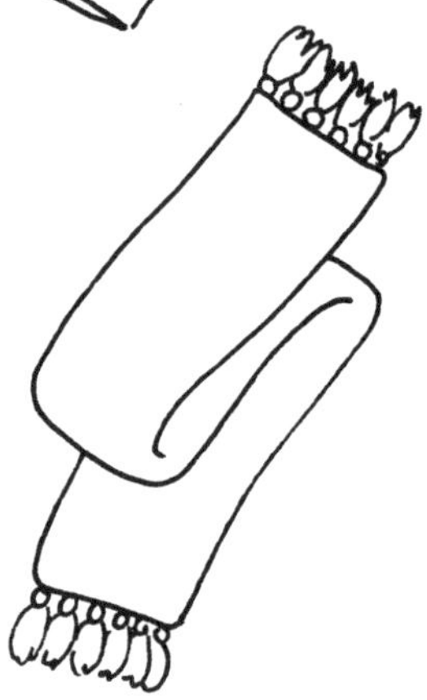

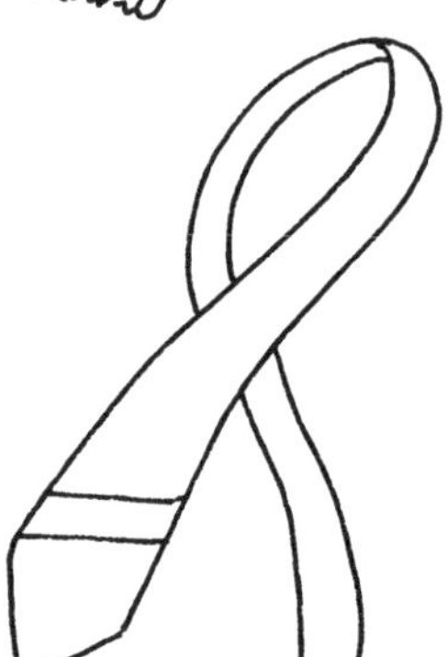

- ○ shoes
- ○ suitcase
- ○ hat
- ○ sunglasses
- ○ handbag
- ○ trousers
- ○ cap
- ○ hat

Can you find the names of five things to wear?

Findest du fünf Dinge zum Anziehen?

a	s	x	s	o	e	m
b	h	w	a	t	c	h
k	o	u	v	i	a	z
	e	w	r	e	p	
	s	c	a	r	f	
	m	u	h	o	p	

Cross out the pictures of the ones you find. What is left?

Welche sind es? Kreuze an. Was bleibt übrig?

baker

Mr. John is a baker.

dentist

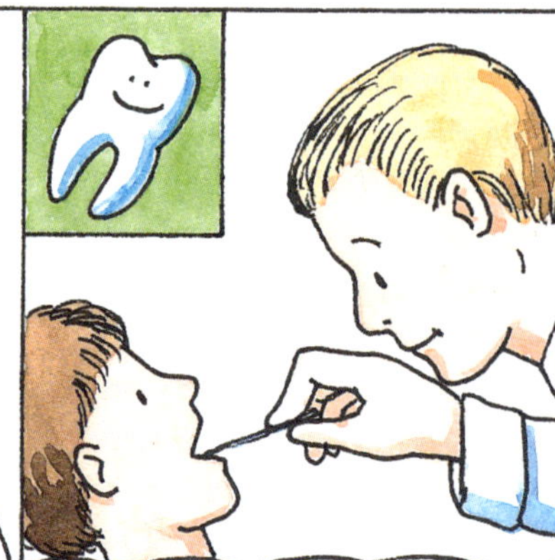

Tom is at the dentist´s.

butcher

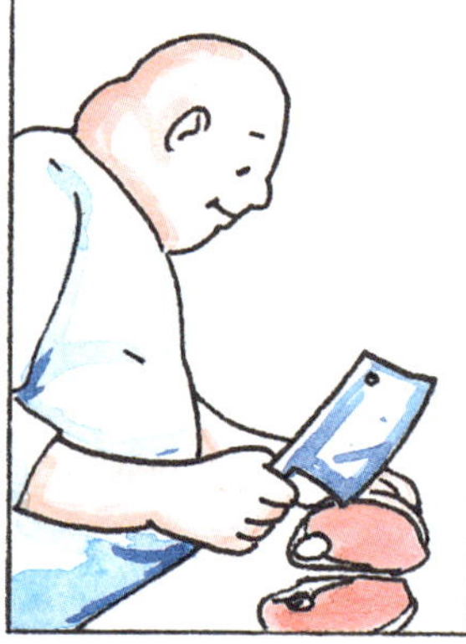

Mr. Pix is a butcher.

doctor

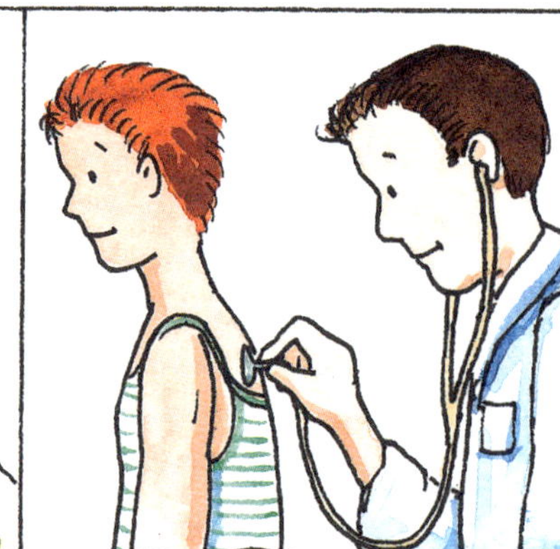

Mr. Brown is a doctor.

cook

Mrs. Pot is a cook.

farmer

Mr. Smith is a farmer.

nurse

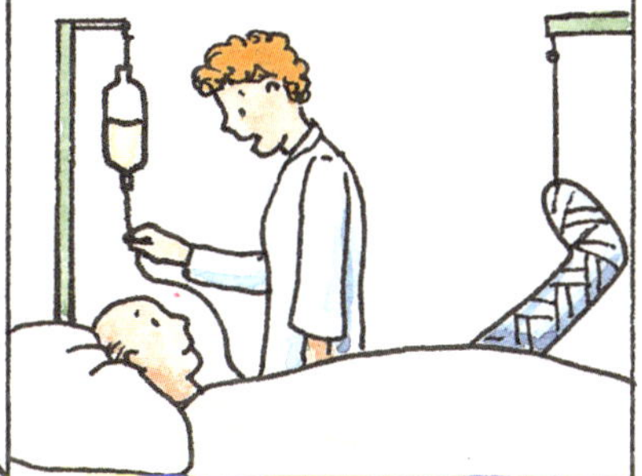

Mrs. Shaw is a nurse in a hospital.

shoemaker

Mr. Black is a shoemaker.

policeman

Mr. Green is a policeman.

tailor

Mr. Hooper is a tailor.

postman

Mr. Letter is a postman.

teacher

Mrs. Miller is a teacher.

Fill in the missing letters.

Welcher Buchstabe fehlt?

d.ct.r

sh.emaker

p.stman

c..k

p.liceman

tail.r

nurs.

bak.r

d.ntist

t.ach.r

butch.r

farm.r

te.cher

t.ilor

f.rmer

b.ker

policem.n

postm.n

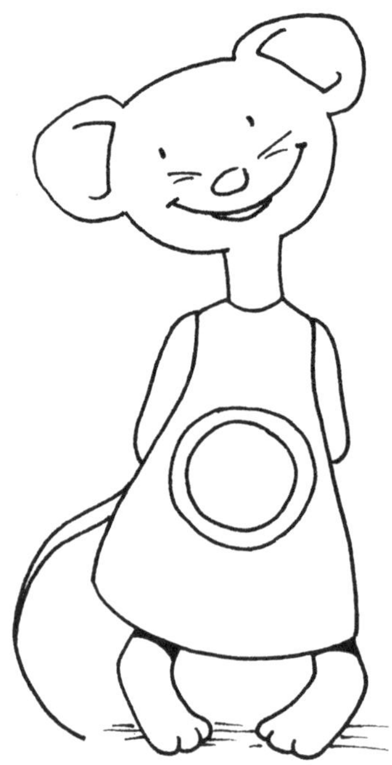

Who needs what?
Join up.

Wer braucht was?
Verbinde!

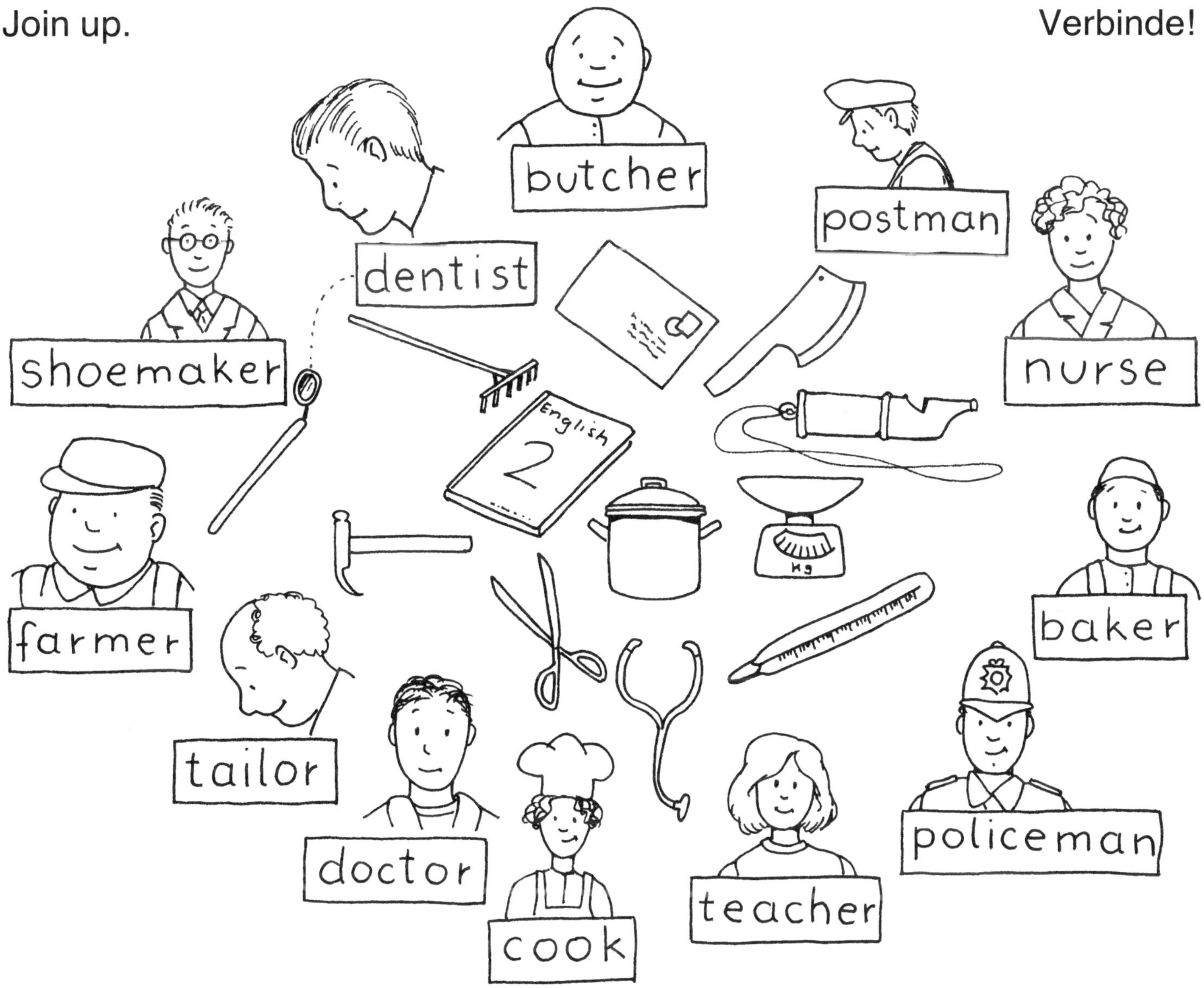

What do you want to be?

Was möchtest du werden?

Furniture

armchair

My armchair is red.

chair

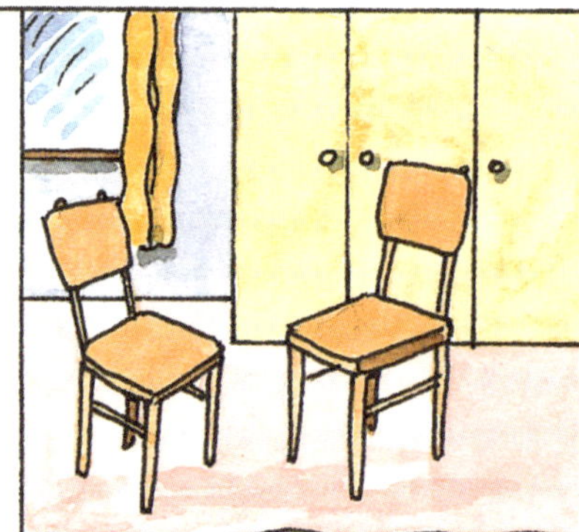

There are two chairs in my room.

bed

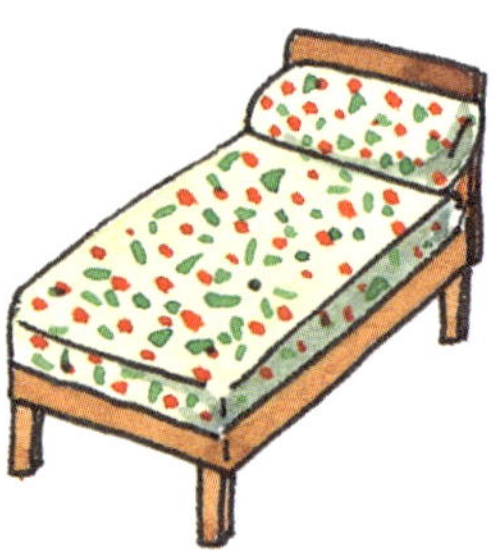

I have a big bed.

clock

There is a clock in my room.

carpet

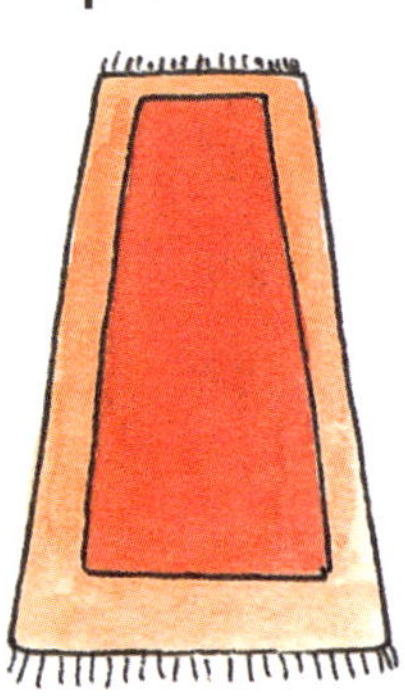

There is a green carpet on the floor.

lamp

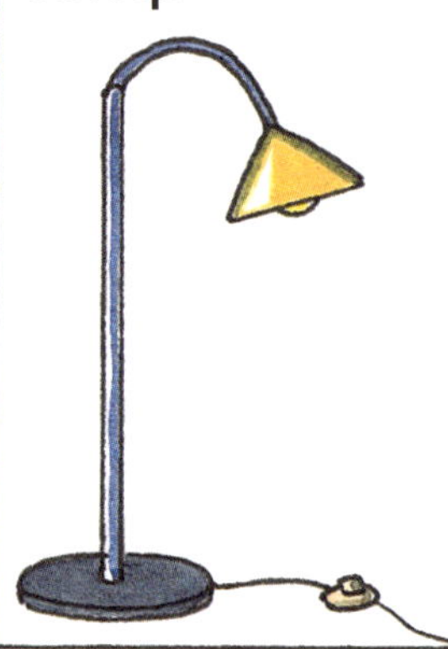

There are two lamps in my room.

radio

I often listen to music on the radio.

table

There is a table in the kitchen.

shelf

There is a shelf on the wall.

television set

I have a small TV set.

sofa

I like to sleep on the sofa.

wardrobe

My clothes hang in the wardrobe.

Furniture

The house is getting painted.
What is under each dustsheet?

Die Maler sind im Haus.
Was steht unter der Plane?

armchair | carpet | chair | wardrobe

tv

lamp

bed

sofa

table | shelf | clock | radio

Where do we put the furniture when the painting is finished?

Wohin müssen die Möbel, wenn die Maler fertig sind?

bedroom

b e d	______________
w r d a o b r e	______________
c a r e p t	______________

bathroom

______________	s e l h f
______________	c i a h r
______________	c o c k l

kitchen

t b l a e	______________
l p a m	______________
r o d a i	______________

sitting room

______________	v t
______________	s f a o
______________	a m r ch i a r

Parts of the body

arm and elbow

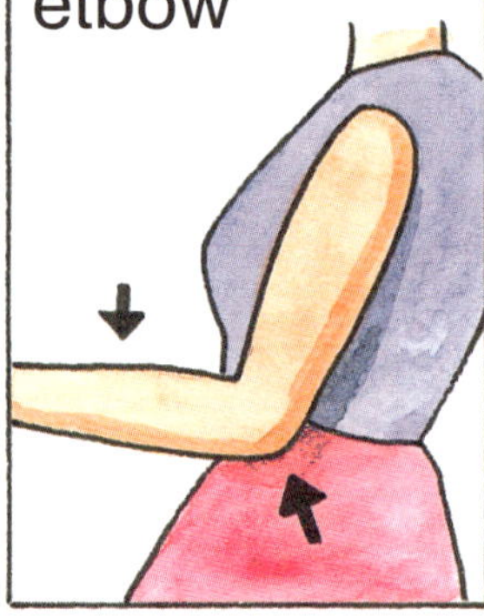

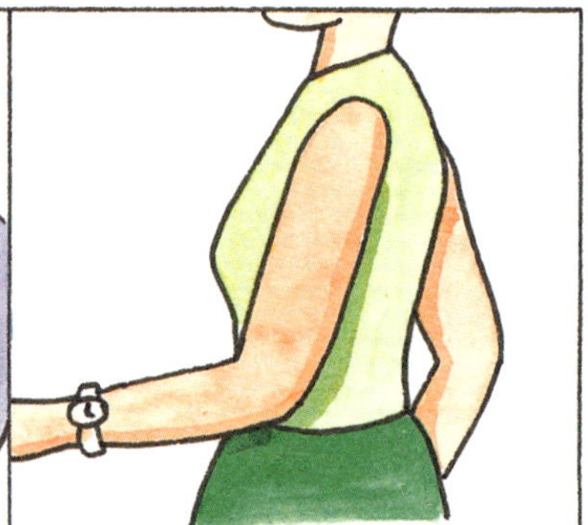

She´s wearing a watch on her arm.

foot and toe

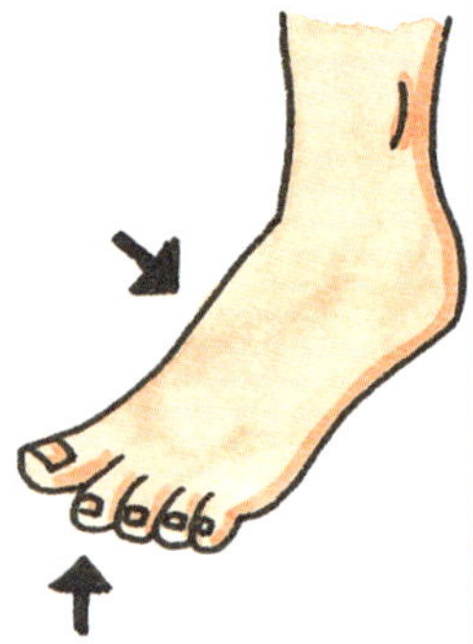

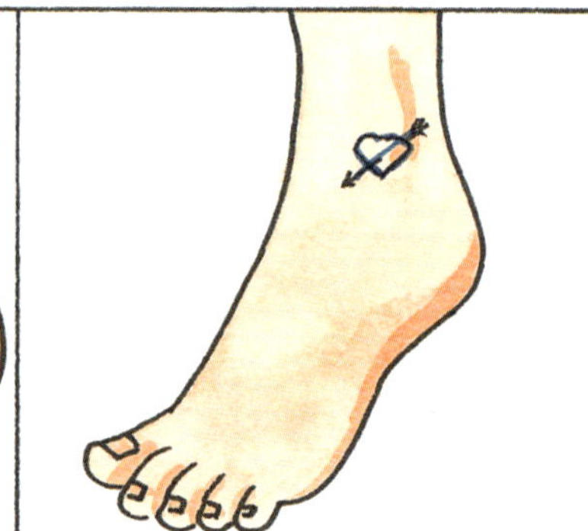

She has a tatoo on her foot.

ear

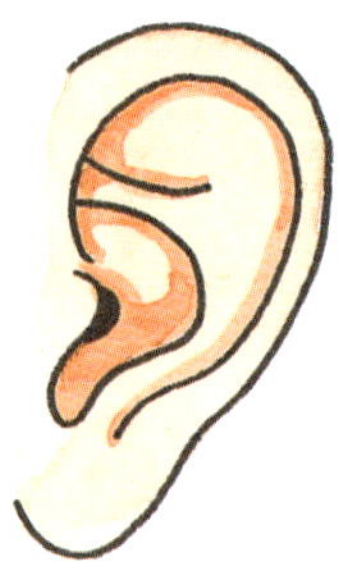

She´s wearing an earring.

hair

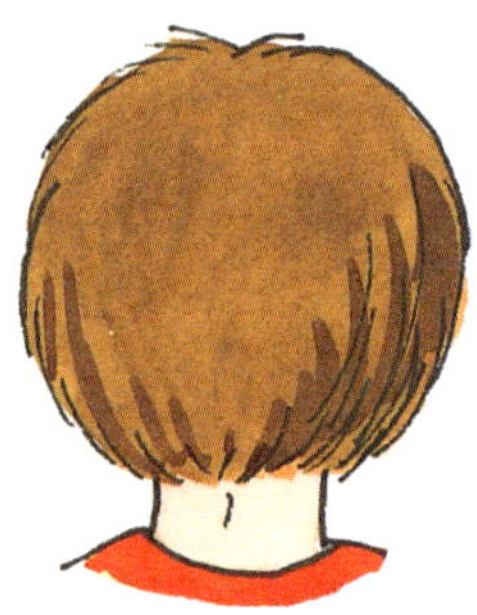

Has she got red hair?
Has she got brown hair?

eye

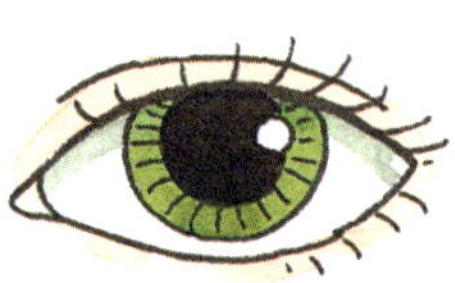

She has got big eyes.

hand with fingers

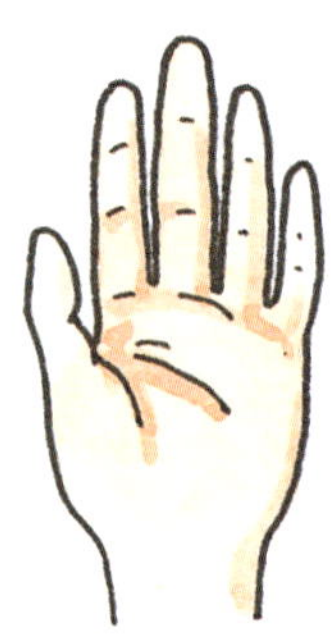

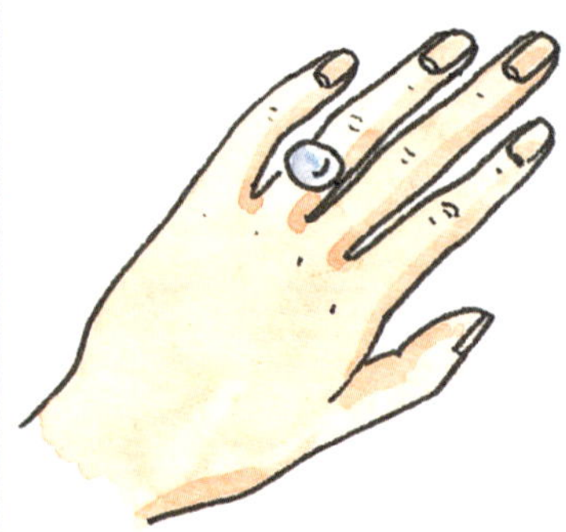

She´s wearing a ring on her hand.

head and face

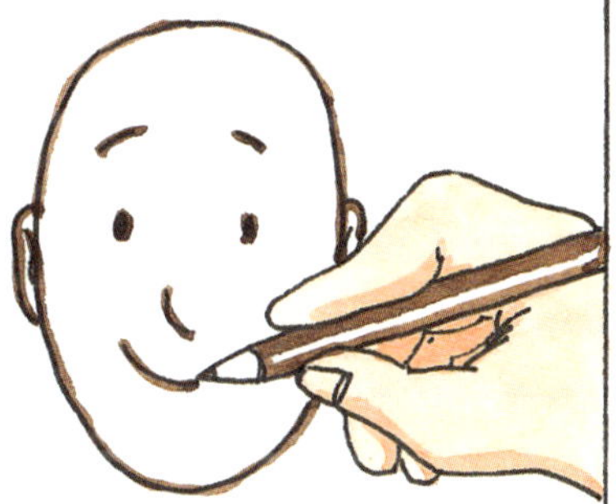

Draw the head first and then draw the face.

neck

She´s wearing a necklace.

leg and knee

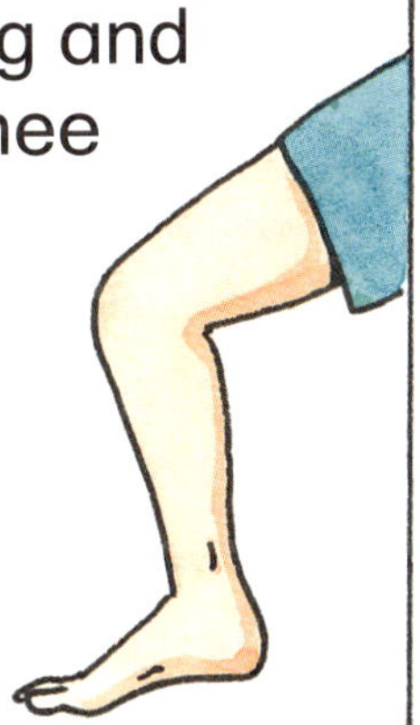

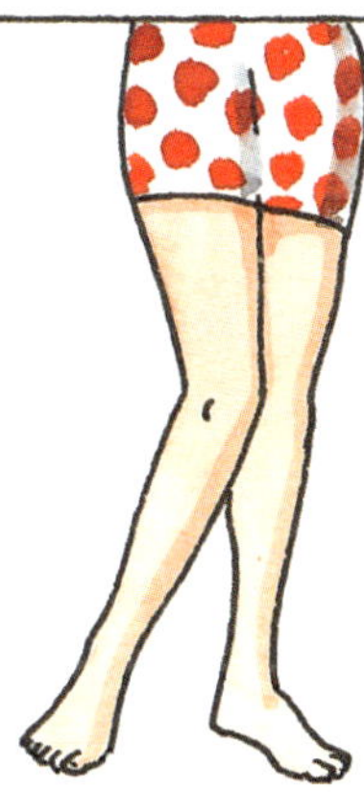

Her legs are long.

nose

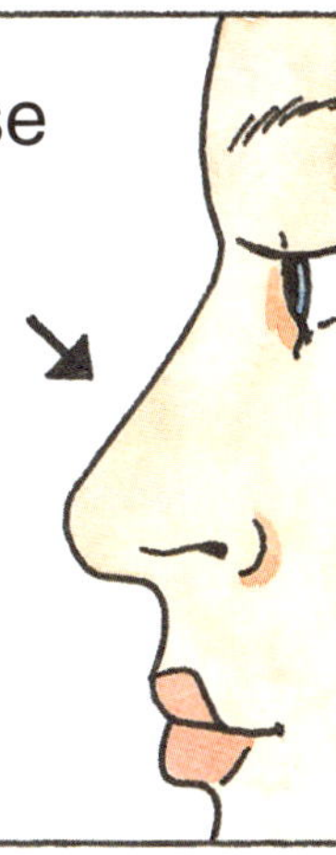

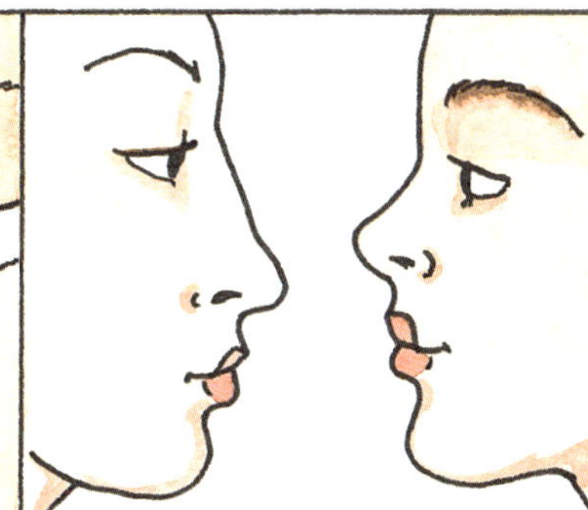

Has she got a long nose? Has she got a short nose?

mouth

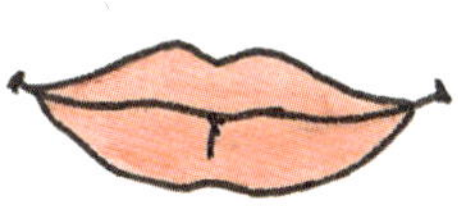

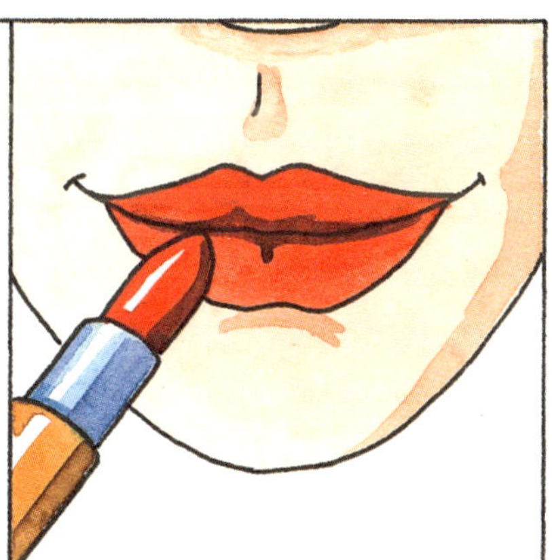

Her mouth is red.

shoulder

She´s wearing a scarf round her shoulders.

What´s missing in these pictures? Join up.

Ein schlechter Fotograf. Was fehlt? Verbinde!

ear

neck

hair

eye

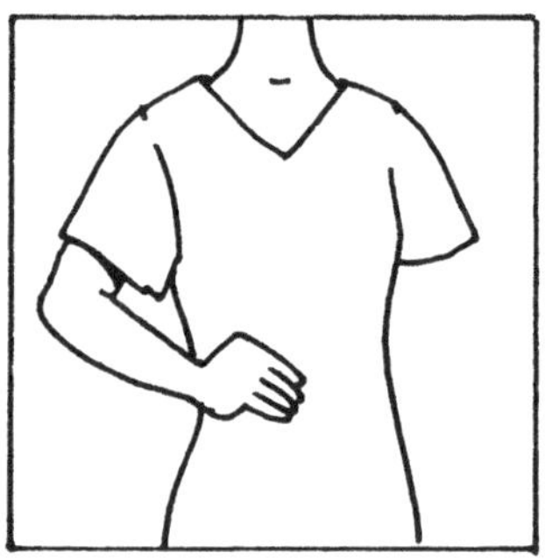

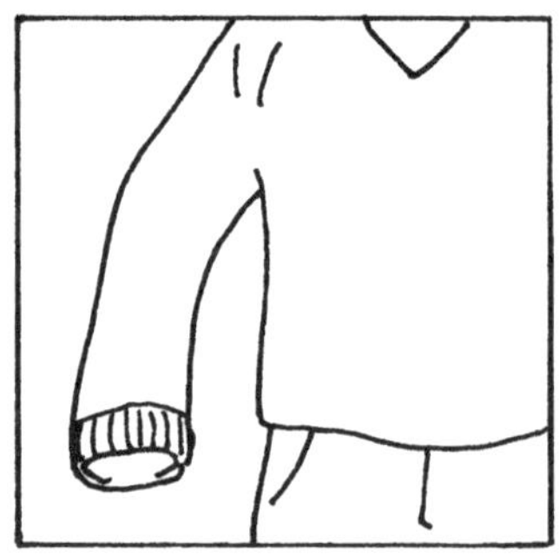

leg

arm

nose

hand

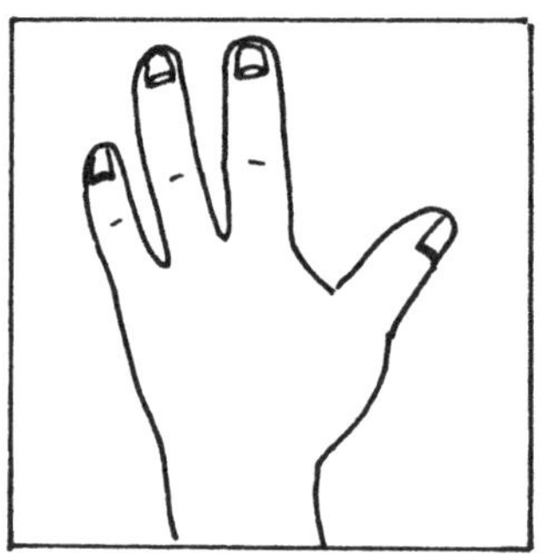

face

finger

Can you read this secret writing?

Fahre die Geheimschriften nach! Was erkennst du?

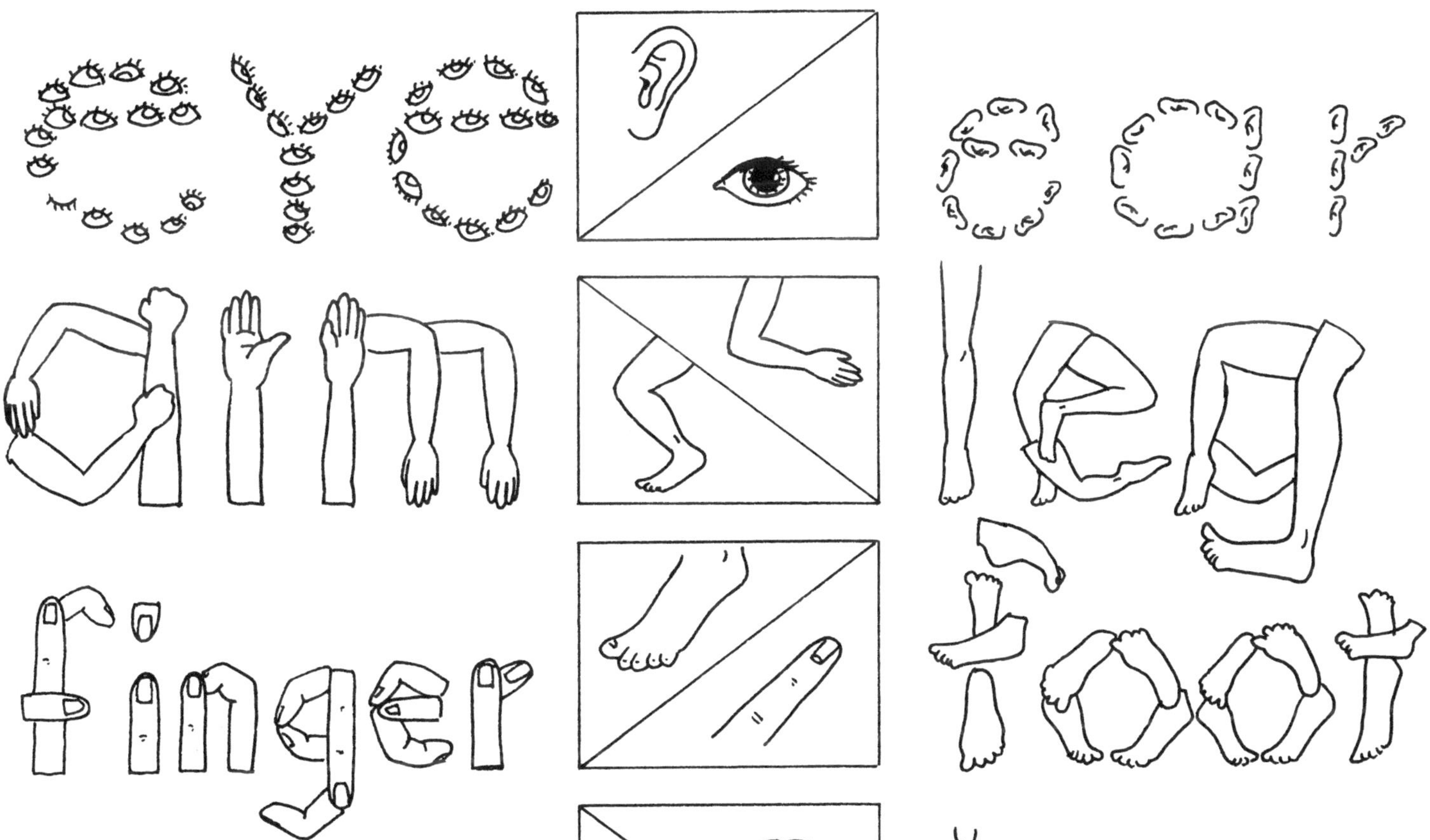

Days of the week and seasons

Monday

The first day of the week

Tuesday

The second day of the week

Wednesday

The third day of the week

Thursday

The fourth day of the week

Friday

The fifth day of the week

Saturday

The sixth day of the week

Tage und Jahreszeiten

Sunday

The seventh day of the week

autumn

Autumn starts on 23rd September.

spring

Spring starts on 20th March.

winter

Winter starts on 21st December.

summer

Summer starts on 21st June.

all together

1 Monday
2 Tuesday
3 Wednesday
4 Thursday
5 Friday
6 Saturday
7 Sunday

Spring
1 20. 3.
Summer
2 21. 6.
Autumn
3 23. 9
Winter
4 21. 12.

What day is missing
on the calendar?

Welcher Tag fehlt
auf dem Kalender?

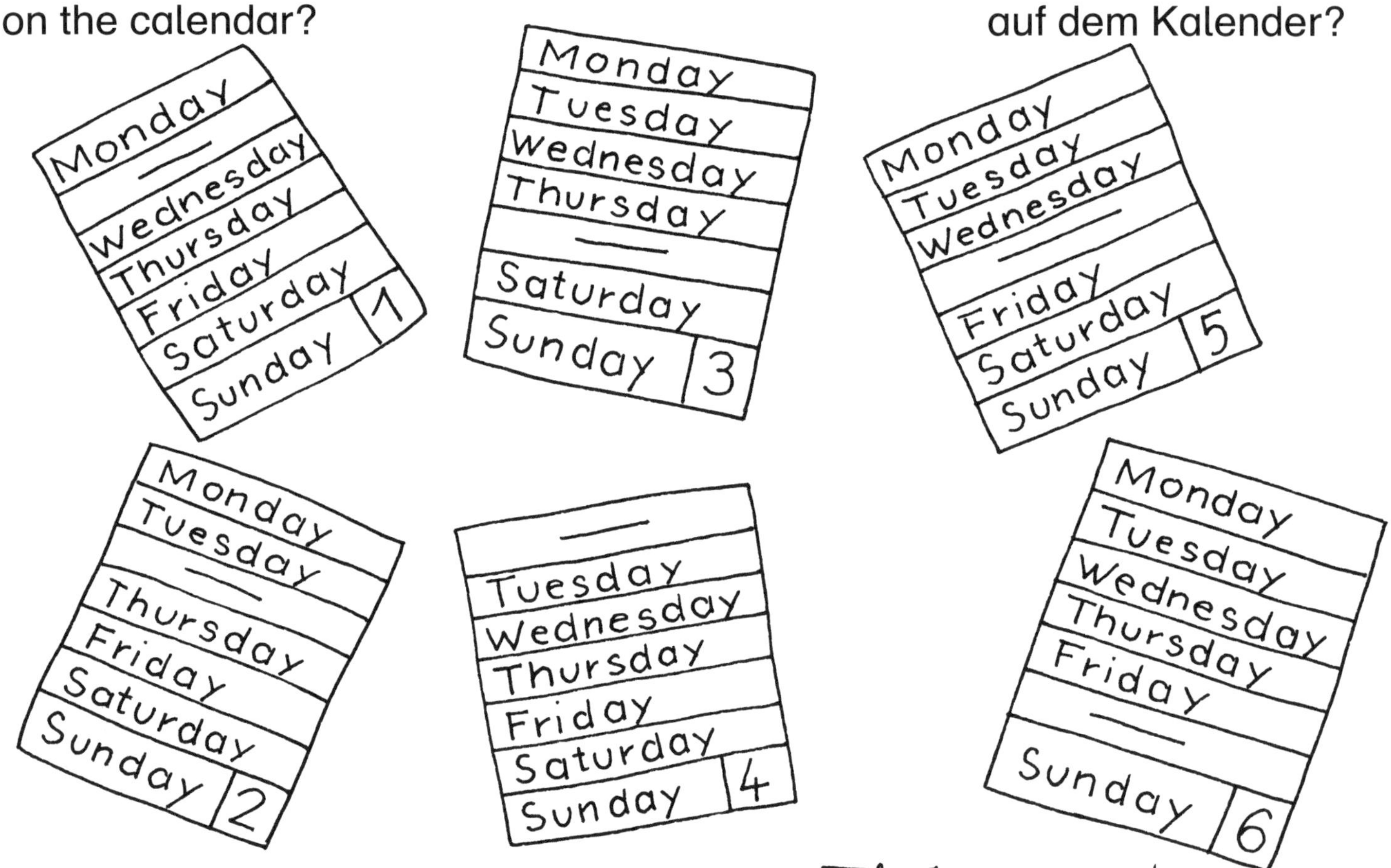

4 Monday

Tuesday

Wednesday

Thursday

Friday

Saturday

Do you know the seasons?

Kennst du die Jahreszeiten?

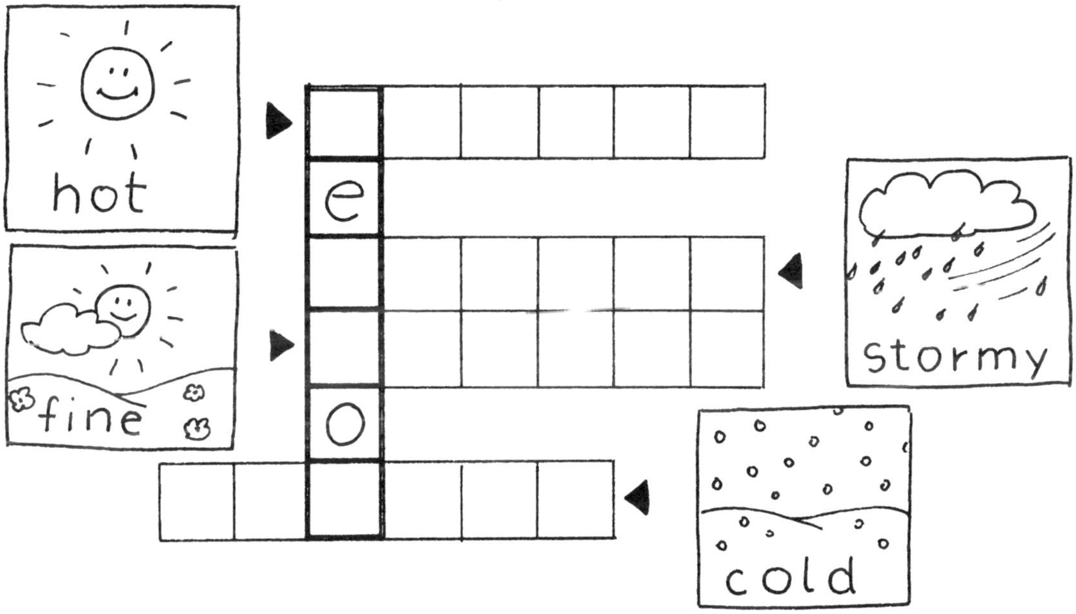

Join up.

Setze zusammen!

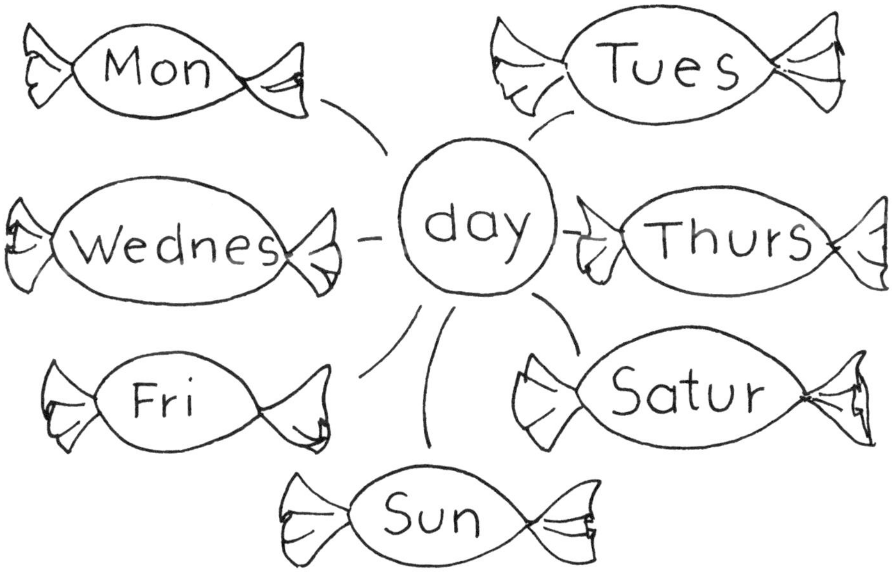

One week:
Eine Woche:

M
T

Months of the year

January

In January it is very cold.

February

February is the shortest month.

March

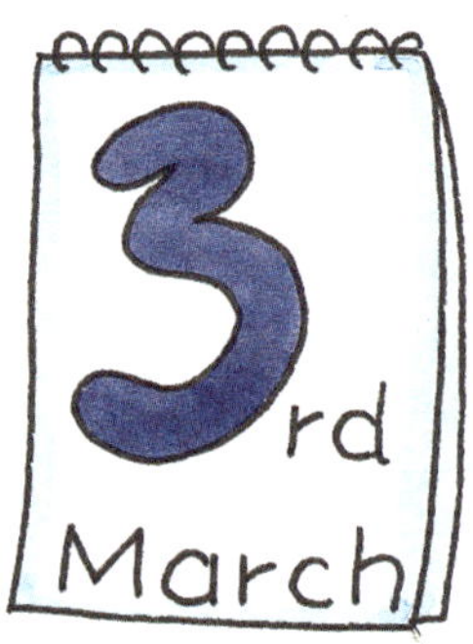

Flowers grow in March.

April

April is a rainy month.

May

May is between April and June.

June

Summer starts in June.

July

We go swimming in July.

August

We go on holiday in August.

September

Autumn starts in September.

October

Hallowe´en is in October.

November

November is a windy month.

December

Christmas is in December.

Mein Vokabeltrainer

Tiere auf dem Bauernhof:
cat: Katze
cow: Kuh
dog: Hund
duck: Ente
fly: Fliege
goose: Gans
hen: Huhn
horse: Pferd
mouse: Maus
pig: Schwein
rabbit: Hase
sheep: Schaf

Tiere im Zoo:
bear: Bär
dolphin: Delfin
elephant: Elefant
giraffe: Giraffe
lion: Löwe
monkey: Affe
parrot: Papagei
penguin: Pinguin
rhinoceros: Nashorn
snake: Schlange
tiger: Tiger
tortoise: Schildkröte

Musikinstrumente:
drum: Trommel
guitar: Gitarre
keyboard: Keyboard
piano: Klavier
recorder: Flöte
trumpet: Trompete

Spielzeuge:
doll: Puppe
jigsaw: Puzzlespiel
kite: Drachen
skipping rope: Springseil
teddy bear: Teddybär
train set: Eisenbahn

Zahlen:
one: eins
two: zwei
three: drei
four: vier
five: fünf
six: sechs
seven: sieben
eight: acht
nine: neun
ten: zehn
zero: null
hundred: hundert

Farben:
black: schwarz
blue: blau
brown: braun
green: grün
grey: grau
orange: orange
pink: rosa
purple: purpurrot
red: rot
white: weiß
yellow: gelb

Schulsachen:
board: Tafel
book: Buch
crayon: Farbstifte
exercise book: Übungsheft
glue: Klebstoff
notebook: Notizbuch
pen: Füller
pencil: Bleistift
rubber: Radiergummi
ruler: Lineal
school bag: Schultasche
scissors: Schere

Obst:
apple: Apfel
banana: Banane
cherry: Kirsche
grapes: Trauben
kiwi fruit: Kiwi
lemon: Zitrone
orange: Orange
peach: Pfirsich
pear: Birne
pineapple: Ananas
strawberry: Erdbeere
water melon: Wassermelone

Fahrzeuge:
bike: Fahrrad
boat: Boot
bus: bus
car: Auto
helicopter: Hubschrauber
motorbike: Motorrad
plane: Flugzeug
scooter: Roller
ship: Schiff
taxi: Taxi
train: Zug
tram: Straßenbahn

Nahrungsmittel:
bread: Brot
butter: Butter
cake: Kuchen
egg: Ei
fish and chips: Fisch und Pommes
ham: Schinken
cheese: Käse
jam: Marmelade
honey: Honig
sausages: Würstchen
spaghetti: Spagetti
pizza: Pizza
soup: Suppe
breakfast: Frühstück
lunch: Mittagessen
dinner: Abendessen

Getränke:
beer: Bier
champagne: Champagner
coffee: Kaffee
coke: Coca Cola
fizzy water: Mineralwasser
hot chocolate: heiße Schokolade
juice: Saft
lemonade: Limonade
milk: Milch
tea: Tee
whisky: Whisky
wine: Wein